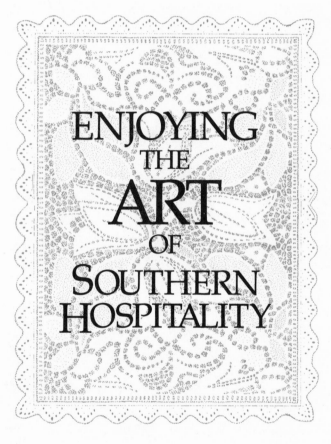

ENJOYING
THE
ART
OF
SOUTHERN
HOSPITALITY

ENJOYING
T H E
Art
of
SOUTHERN
HOSPITALITY

MENUS,
RECIPES
AND
SUGGESTIONS
FOR
ENTERTAINING
SIMPLY
AND
GRACIOUSLY

Sara Pitzer

August House Publishers, Inc.
LITTLE ROCK

Published by August House, Inc.,
P.O. Box 3223, Little Rock, Arkansas, 72203,
501–372–5450.

Printed in the United States of America

10 9 8 7 6 5 4 3 2 1

LIBRARY OF CONGRESS CATALOGING-IN-PUBLICATION DATA

Pitzer, Sara.
Enjoying the art of Southern hospitality : menus, recipes, and suggestions
for entertaining simply and graciously / Sara Pitzer.—1st ed.
p. cm.
Includes bibliographic references and index.
ISBN 0-87483-121-0 (alk. paper)
1. Cookery, American—Southern style. 2. Menus. I. Title.
TX715.2.S68P58 1990
641.5975—dc20   90-46504

First Edition, 1990

Executive editor: Liz Parkhurst
Design director: Ted Parkhurst
Book design: Communication Graphics
Cover design and interior illustrations: Kitty Harvill
Typography: Lettergraphics, Little Rock, AR

AUGUST HOUSE, INC.   PUBLISHERS   LITTLE ROCK

DEDICATION

This is for Croy, whose hospitality is intuitive and impeccable, and for Ted and Liz, who put the fun back into publishing for me.

C O N T E N T S

What Makes Hospitality Southern?

Ind why is it Southern hospitality that is famous? People give parties in San Diego, invite friends for dinner in Cincinnati, serve desserts and coffee in Philadelphia, celebrate New Year's Eve in Kansas City, so why not fame for West Coast hospitality or Eastern hospitality or Midwestern hospitality? Why Southern hospitality? In studying historic accounts, literary references and contemporary stories about hospitality in the South, I found a surprising answer.

I believe many people share the notion I once had that Southern hospitality somehow always centered around elegance, opulence, and excess. Sometimes that's what it *has* meant—especially as practiced by hosts and hostesses of the upper class during the years from after the Revolution until the Civil War—and some old accounts certainly support the sense that all was opulence, elaborately decorated plantation dining rooms, mountains of food, armies of servants, and rivers of bourbon and champagne.

Henry Barnard, for instance, visited the Carter family near Petersburg, Virginia, in 1833, and later described a meal which began with the ladies being led formally by the gentlemen into the dining room, where servants proceeded to serve a lavish meal beginning with soup, followed by five kinds of meat and many vegetables. Champagne was poured freely. After this came at least six different desserts. And then, as recounted in Dixon Wecter's *Saga of American Society,* poor Mr. Barnard reports in what may have been either dismay or astonishment:

> ...off goes the second table cloth, and then upon the bare
> mahogany table is set, the figs, raisins, and almonds, and
> before Mr. Carter is set 2 or 3 bottles of wine—Maderia,
> Port, and a sweet wine for the Ladies—he fills his glass,
> and pushes them on, after the glasses are filled, the gen-
> tlemen pledge their services to the Ladies and down goes
> the wine, aftr the first and second glass the ladies retire,
> and the gentlemen begin to circulat the bottle pretty
> briskly.

Similarly, in his introduction to the little *Receipt Book of Harriott Pinck-ney Horry, 1770,* Richard J. Hooker writes about a dinner Harriot had at the

home of Major Gibbons, entertaining an Episcopalian bishop. The dinner, which she called "very nice," included goose, ham, tongue, cauliflower, potatoes, salads, peas, green beans, sturgeon, chicken, veal, and for dessert, ice cream, strawberries, pudding, preserved gooseberries, and white heart cherries. If that meal was merely nice, one wonders what a stupendous dinner might have been.

But everyone did not entertain that way, nor did society necessarily expect it. In 1839, Mrs. Lettice Bryan wrote this advice in *The Kentucky Housewife*: "Just try to learn what your company is fondest of, and have their favorites. A few things well ordered will never fail to give a greater appetite, and pleasure to your guest, than a crowded table badly prepared...."

Even during the high times, not all Southerners were fabulously wealthy. Food sources were never uniformly prolific throughout the South. In pioneering days, frontier families offered guests whatever food they had for themselves, usually a variety of game, corn breads, and whatever fruits and vegetables they had. It seems likely that when a housewife realized she wouldn't have enough wild turkey to feed the guests and family, she might get out the leftovers and bake an additional kind of bread to extend the meal.

During the dark days following the Civil War, in particular, successful hostesses made much of little and created a festive atmosphere with the illusion of plenty. In *Mary Chesnut's Civil War Diary*, edited by C. Vann Woodward, she describes a typical bill of fare for supper: "Wild turkey, wild ducks, partridges, oysters, and a bowl of apple toddy made by Mrs. Davis's recipe." Probably she hadn't enough of any one thing to feed everyone, but by serving this variety she not only produced enough food for a party, but also evoked overtones of earlier lavish dinners.

In account after account, we find this—that what mattered wasn't the trappings, but the party itself. In *Journal of a Secesh Lady: The Diary of Catherine Ann Devereux 1860 to 1866*, we read: "Came Mr. Brinkley to dinner .... Had our pudding in honour of the day, the 11th of Feb, & in the afternoon Mr E insisted on opening one of our few remaining bottles of wine which I have been hoarding for an emergenc. The taste of the fine dry old sherry with its rich bouquet & nutty flavour carried us back to past & the blessing we then enjoyed."

Another fascinating example of the Southern determination to have a good time in spite of hardship comes from Cleora Butler, a talented cook and caterer. In *Cleora's Kitchens*, she wrote about the effects of the crash of October 1929 on entertaining among black and white people in Tulsa, saying that money had already become tight in her black community:

> Still everyone loved parties and a good time as much
> as they ever did...Our way around this was for everyone
> to bring something. We'd get together and brew our own
> beer. Then each would bring his or her share of ingredi-

ents for the planned menu. It always turned out to be an exciting evening.

After the bottom dropped out, the well-to-do (and not a few of the wealthy) followed our example. Mr. and Mrs. Snedden were part of a group of twelve couples who gathered periodically for dinner, sharing proportionately the cost of the evening.

Recently, in the same spirit, Freddy Arnaud, of an old, party-loving family in New Orleans, made elaborate plans to celebrate his father's eightieth birthday. He was planning a huge dinner on a riverboat, complete with a renowned jazz band. Then the serious illness of another family member made the celebration Freddy had planned inappropriate. So, he reserved a private dining room at Antoine's for a smaller celebration instead. He said, "I told the family, we have to have *some* party."

The same impulse prompted a couple renovating an old house in Natchez a few years ago. Their house wasn't fixed up yet, but they had a party anyway. The only heat came from two fireplaces, the only light from candles. Cobwebs still clung to the old paintings on the walls and the antique rosewood furniture was pushed back to barricade broken spots in the floors. Guests had to bring their own liquor. But everybody understood. The owners needed a party.

A look at the history of Southern hospitality suggests that the one true constant is this passion for a party. Bad times or good, the South will have parties. From frontier days until today, Southerners have worked around difficulties and deprivations in order to entertain. Only the nature of the impediments changes. We read about parties in Washington D.C. after the Civil War at which the only refreshment was plates of chipped ice, and about debutante balls in Charleston and Savannah during Reconstruction where there was nothing to drink but water. But they had the parties.

Today's challenge is different. The frontier is settled and paved, the war and its privations past. Today, we have plenty of food but little help in preparing and serving it. We have the knowledge that the traditional old foods tend to carry quantities of fat, sugar, and salt that our mostly sedentary bodies shouldn't have. We have comfortable homes but limited space for guests.

No question, these are new challenges.

In our parties today, we can't emulate the grand spreads of plantation prosperity, nor can we get away with the Reconstruction simplicity of serving ice and water. In our fast-paced, servantless, trimmed-down times, our challenge is to find new ways of continuing the old spirit of Southern parties. The following chapter looks at the three essential elements of Southern hospitality and suggests how you can evoke them in today's entertaining.

1

The
Spirit
of
Southern
Hospitality
Today

O   h, don't go to any trouble for *me*," may be the most dishonest
           words we utter. We hesitate to admit this because we fear that
           people won't like us if we're too much trouble, but we really do
enjoy seeing signs that our hosts and hostesses have taken the trouble to
make things special because we're there.

Magazines now routinely publish articles on how to make your home
seem more like a country inn for guests when, originally, the success of
country inns grew from their seeming like home for people who had to
travel. If we think about some of the things that make those inns so
popular—cookies upon arrival, flowers in the guest rooms, and innkeep-
ers who remember from one visit to the next whether we prefer dark or
light turkey meat—we have some clues about how we can recapture a
sense of hospitality in our own lives and homes.

Three specific elements make people feel welcome: ceremony, personal attention, and good (but not necessarily extravagant) food. These are
all ways of focusing on our guests, the core spirit of Southern entertaining.

Using ceremonies to transform ordinary experience into festivity is
part of the genius of Southern entertaining. Rob Kuehnle, a native of
Natchez, wrote a column for *Mississippi* magazine describing a ritual that
made cutting a watermelon at the end of Sunday dinner a festivity the
children have remembered ever since. They called it "presentation of the
watermelon." Kuehnle writes that it was like a little play. The grandfather
always carried the melon to the front porch, led the children in a dance,
and finally cut the melon, a little at a time, hoping aloud that it would be
good and not have to go to the pigs. Of course the melon was always wonderful. "The entire ritual was designed to wring every bit of drama and
excitement from what would have been, for most people, an ordinary
experience," Kuehnle wrote.

Another bit of genius is the Southern understanding, that once
seemed almost intuitive, of knowing how to focus on guests to make them
feel welcome, relaxed, and celebratory. Mrs. Lettice Bryan said it clearly
back in 1839 in *The Kentucky Housewife* when she admonished hostesses
just to learn what their guests were fondest of and have their favorites.
Author Celestine Sibley, in her book, *A Place Called Sweet Apple*, said it
most simply, quoting a neighbor: "You just come and spend a spell with
Ida Belle and me. We'll treat you so many different ways one of 'em is
bound to suit you."

At first it sounds almost silly. When you entertain, aren't you by defi-
nition focusing on your guests? A glance at some of the current books
about entertaining suggests otherwise. Color photographs show tables
and counters overflowing with artfully arranged, elaborately garnished
food. Myriad dishes of bright vegetables set off roasts. Perfect cakes and
pies flank baskets of gleaming fruits. Glasses of wine sparkle. It all looks
too good to eat. To confirm your suspicion that the food is for photograph-
ing, not eating, you'll see no people in the pictures eating anything.
Indeed, you'll see no people. As John Thorne, the editor and writer of the

Simple Cooking newsletter, observes, the pictures represent artful examples of do-it-yourself catering. Catering isn't the same as hospitable entertaining. Catering implies preparing foor *for* someone; entertaining means the more personal act of sharing it *with* them. Thorne refers to a real party, as opposed to a catered event, as a "joint conspiracy" in a good time. It's hard to focus on your guests when you're worrying about the garnishes on your *grillades*.

As so many historic and contemporary recollections of parties show, guests enjoy an attentive host and hostess as much as they enjoy their food, but that doesn't mean the food doesn't matter. Elaborate food is not necessary. Good food is; and these days that means simple food. Nothing else really leaves a hostess free to concentrate on her guests. The elaborate old menus and recipes were, to put it mildly, labor intensive. Cooks, servants, and even gardeners made it all possible. The hostess supervised, but basically, at party time, she was free to be with the guests, knowing the food would be brought to the table.

Two stories illustrate this humorously. In her introduction to the reprint of *Two Hundred Years of Charleston Cooking,* Elizabeth Verner Hamilton writes about a young Charleston bride during World War I who decided to rent her home to a Navy wife and live with her parents until the war was over and her husband came home. The Navy wife loved the house but called the mother of the Charleston bride to say that she couldn't possibly rent the house until something was done about the kitchen. After a long, shocked silence, the mother said, "You *went* into the kitchen?"

Equally telling, the introduction written by Darlene Roth for the reprint of the *Atlanta Exposition Cookbook* suggests that many of the women who contributed recipes for the cookbook never cooked. One of them reported she had tried it once and found it so devastating she never cooked again.

It's easy to focus on your guests ceremoniously when someone else is focusing on the kitchen. The question is, how can we do both?

What does it mean, really, to focus on guests? It means, quite simply, doing something special because they are there, without giving them the sense that we're afraid our efforts won't be good enough or out of sorts because we're exhausted from getting ready for them. The inns put fancy soaps in your bathroom and fresh flowers on your bedside table. The at-home possibilities are nicer. No one understood this better than the Hampton sisters, who served as hostesses for their father, Wade Hampton II, at Millwood, in Columbia, South Carolina. When folks were in such bad shape they could scarcely put food on their tables, the sisters gave the preacher a tablecloth. The story is told by an exhibit label on the Reverend Shand's tablecloth at the Hampton–Preston Mansion, now a museum, in Columbia.

The Legend of the Tablecloth

The War Between the States brought deprivation to everyone in Columbia. However, even among the ruins, people made an effort to maintain a polite society. For example, the Hampton sisters discovered that the rector of Trinity Episcopal Church, the Reverend Peter Shand, was dining off a bare table. They presented him with the tablecloth shown here which was made from a bolt of linen ordered by Wade Hampton II from Ireland for Millwood Plantation. The state symbol, a palmetto tree, is woven into the border.

Never again did the reverend have to entertain at dinner from a bare table.

Of course there's more to it than tablecloths, but what a tablecloth stands for is important—the extra effort to make things nice. You can manage it lots of ways. The old-time, money-is-no-object way might be professional floral arrangements, damask cloths, sterling flatware, and crystal glasses. Today's realistic counterpart, which clearly communicates more of your personal involvement, might be a handful of wildflowers or ivy cuttings or autumn leaves displayed in a pitcher.

It's not a new idea. Reminiscing about party suppers in her book, *Dishes & Beverages of the Old South,* Martha McCulloch–Williams wrote in 1913, "… often the table was gay with autumn leaves, the centerpiece a riot of small ragged red chrysanthemums, or raggeder pink or yellow ones …" In the same chapter she extolled the beauty of oranges with the peel cut to took like lilies and the fun of punches decorated with cuttings of apple skins and orange peels, all special decorations created quickly from materials at hand. To show today's guests that you've taken that kind of thought, let polyester suffice for the tablecloth, and an assortment of candles from the grocery store surrounded with flowers or greenery cut from the yard or park can serve as the "special" decorations.

One of the prettiest adaptations of this idea I've ever seen was at a springtime luncheon where the main decoration—on a simple white-clothed table set in blue and white china—was pansies floating in small brandy snifters at each place. A similar approach graced an afternoon dessert party on Valentine's Day. The hostess worked until an hour or two before the party and obviously didn't have a lot of time to fuss with decorations, so she set the buffet table with a white cloth and her everyday white stoneware. For decoration, she lit red candles (left over from Christmas) and scattered heart candies and grade-school valentines among the sweets.

I remember a time nearly three decades ago when sheer necessity forced me into this kind of inventiveness. At the time I wasn't crazy about the situation, but now I'm rather proud of myself. We belonged to a little

group of people who decided to take turns preparing "experimental gourmet" dinners. The cooking didn't worry me; I'd been doing that since I was twelve and I figured that as long as I served something other than spaghetti and meatballs I could call it "experimental."

The trouble, as I saw it then, was that the other couples were considerably ahead of us in acquisitions. They had dining rooms; we had only an eat-in kitchen. They had sterling flatware; I had stainless. They had bone china; I had Corningware, the kind with a blue fleurs-de-lis design on the edges. Worse yet, they had damask and linen tablecloths and napkins; I had one blue tablecloth, period. We used paper napkins and folded paper towels.

I was wandering through a variety store, trying to figure out something to save myself, when I came upon a display of red bandanas, the kind farmers wipe their brows with and California yuppies tie around the necks of their dogs. The bandanas were on sale—sixty-nine cents each. I figured it out, six times sixty-nine. That came to $4.14. I kind of hated to spend it; that was, after all, the better part of a five-dollar bill. But it seemed as though I should splurge a bit for my first experimental gourmet dinner party.

Once set, the table looked quite, and appropriate to the kitchen. The red, white and blue of the bandana/napkins and Corningware dishes were laid out on a matching blue tablecloth. I'd sneaked a handful of daisies ouf of a neighbor's yard the night before and arranged them in a white pitcher with long stems of mint as foliage.

We started out a little stiff and ill at ease, but then one of the men made a really bad joke about using his bandana as a handkerchief, and we all started laughing and making more bad jokes and ended up having a howling good time until well past midnight. I still remember it as one of the best dinner parties I ever gave.

No matter how simple or fancy the decorations, once guests arrive, it's still your personal attention that matters most to them. No successful Southern hostess ever said, "Oh, just sit anywhere," or asked another guest to answer the door. Greeting each guest personally as he or she arrives and showing that you've thought about how you will mix people are basics from the earliest days. The old tradition of leading the ladies into the dining room would look a little silly at a dinner for six in a condo dining area, but you can retain the spirit of things with handwritten place cards to indicate that you've given thought to arranging everyone for good conversation.

Small, handwritten menus with the date, occasion, and hosts' names at each place are another pleasant touch. If you can't spare the time to write them for every guest, make one good copy and duplicate it on nice stock on a plain-paper copy machine. In candlelight who is going to notice that they're looking at copies?

And now, as in the days of the *Kentucky Housewife*, learning what your

guests are fondest of and working some of these favorites into the menu speaks volumes about your interest in their having a good time.

As for ceremonial service, you really can't be whipping off one table-cloth after another, carving roasts and ladling soups from two ends of the table, or passing three or four wine bottles at the end of a meal, but we have options that duplicate the spirit. Appetizer plates set on top of dinner plates, placemats removed to expose the tablecloth before dessert and coffee, extra napkins with messy courses, and moist, microwave-warmed, lemon-scented finger towels at the end of the meal give a similar sense of elegant and graceful dining.

You can further develop a sense of ceremony and personal attention at your parties with entertainment—almost a forgotten concept in these days when television rules the parlor. The grand old big parties included danc-ing and music; the smaller ones had everything from parlor games and music to recitation and reading aloud. Sometimes the ladies rehearsed and presented plays. Often guests with special talent would take a turn at a musical instrument or singing. When the talent and mood were right, guests would join the performers turning solos into duets and even cho-ruses. In those days, the hostess was not solely responsible for the enter-tainment; Southerners entertained *each other* at parties. It all goes back to John Thorne's observation that guest and hosts should conspire in having a good time.

The possibilities translated into today's parties are tremendous, more so than in the old times because we are no longer constrained by some of the old proprieties and formalities.

The reason you don't see more such activity at parties may be because we're restrained by shyness. Who's ever met a person who didn't think it was fun to sing, play music, and tell stories? But it feels risky to ask guests to abandon their inhibitions and engage in these pleasures with us lest they think we're corny, hokey, not cool, unsophisticated. When you think about it, who ever had any fun being cool, sophisticated, and uninvolved? If you have the courage to set the example with your entertainment plans, your guests will participate with glee. The party that taught me this truth happened long before I would have been brave enough to ask guests to do something like sing after dinner.

I was lucky enough to have guests who were smarter than I was. One of them showed up for what I'd planned as a fairly formal dinner lugging an amplifier and speaker. His wife carried his electric guitar, an instrument that at the time I considered absolutely without class. I remember chang-ing my plans after dessert with some misgiving to serve coffee and liqueurs in the living room instead of at the table. Speed plugged in his guitar and ran through a few chords as we settled around him. Shortly we were belting out chorus after chorus of "Rocky Top," "The Yellow Rose of Texas," and "Stand by Your Man." High-heeled shoes came off, ties were draped over the backs of chairs, and a few waistband buttons were opened

as we sang on. The next day I received phone calls complimenting me on the best party ever. I never once admitted that the music had been Speed's idea, not mine.

A similar episode with an accordion-playing friend sealed my understanding of the fact that if a host or a smart guest has the nerve to give everyone permission to be uncool they will romp with gusto. I had been taught such disdain for the accordion that I called it a "squeezebox." Yet there we were, all dressed up in my living room again, with a guest so slight she seemed smaller than her accordion leading us into the late hours as we sang our hearts out. The electric guitar and the accordion still aren't my favorite instruments, unless they're what my guests play. Then I think they're the most fun that can be had.

Learn about the talents of your guests and conspire with them ahead of time to entice the people at your parties to entertain each other. Don't stop with music. Storytelling and the nearly lost art of reading aloud can make wonderful parties, too. (See p. 193 in the appendices for a list of books that make especially good party readings.) As with music, arrange it ahead of time with some of the guests so that no one is thrown into panic at the idea of having to perform on the spur of the moment. But others won't mind at all, and since lots of people enjoy reading and telling stories, allow for volunteers on the spot as well. I've discovered in teaching my English classes that people also enjoy reading light poetry aloud in unison, too.

I remember a great party at which we all ended up in front of the fireplace playing what I had always thought of as a church-camp game—the progressive story. The leader begins telling a story, then stops at a point of action to allow the next person to carry on. It had been fun when I was a kid at camp, but it was even more fun when, as adults, we stirred our various experiences and grown-up humor into one big story, something like Chaucer's *Canterbury Tales*, except that no one had to be the nun. And no one had to bear the burden of making up an entire story.

Reading all this you'll perhaps wonder about color slides, home movies, and videocassettes. I don't think they're a good idea, generally. For one thing, you can't get past the clichés about sleeping through Uncle Ed's Bermuda vacation slides. Also, the technology of dim lights, screens, projectors, and VCRs puts us back into the role of spectators rather than participants.

The entertainments I've suggested don't replace good conversation; they supplement it. In this age of television and radio talk shows, having some other kind of fun gives guests a respite from all that talk and insures the health of your party by not making it dependent on conversation alone. For a guest, being given the opportunity for such play can be a wonderfully carefree kind of personal attention.

In addition to personal attention and ceremony, we've identified good food as an important part of a party. Not necessarily fancy food and not necessarily in gargantuan quantities. Just good.

Some of the best party food I've ever eaten was based mainly on zucchini and ground beef. My friend, Ann McCormack, has always had an astonishing number of friends, and she'd invited what seemed like the immediate world to dinner. I didn't see how she was going to do it. Her husband, Jack, had recently given up his job to return to graduate school, cutting their income to a painfully low figure. They were living in a farmhouse where the dining room and living room, warmed in winter only by a wood-burning cookstove, were joined as one room. It didn't look to me as though she had the space or money to give a dinner party for a couple dozen people.

But Ann is a true Southerner by birth and experience. She borrowed card tables to supplement her large dining table and covered them all with matching sheets. To prepare the meal, she peeled, cooked and mashed a huge pot of potatoes fresh from her garden. She fried several pounds of hamburger, combined it with fresh tomatoes and zucchini, also from her garden, and baked it in big lasagna pans until the vegetables were tender and the mixture was fragrant and juicy.

Having kept aside some uncooked zucchinis and tomatoes, she arranged them in baskets as table centerpieces. At the end of the evening, she encouraged her guests to take the decorations home with them.

After a first course of garden lettuce, radishes and green onions, we heaped mashed potatoes on our plates and smothered the potatoes with the zucchini concoction. It was so good that we all ate shameful amounts, which we washed down with red jug wine. I make it a point to prepare and serve the same meal at least once every summer to celebrate how good simple food can be.

Good food, simply prepared, is what the rest of this book is about. First, I offer menus for all kinds of special occasions, from breakfasts to dessert parties. You can use them by consulting the recipes I've called for or by substituting other recipes to fit your own taste and style. The recipes are for good, comfortable Southern favorites (de-fatted and simplified as much as possible) that can be prepared quickly and easily, and served simply without extra help. Many of the recipes can be prepared ahead of time or in stages so that you have little last-minute cooking to do. They are all intended to taste good in a familiar way rather than to titillate tastebuds with exotic flavors. Seasonings are specified for the medium levels of intensity that seem to please most of us most of the time, but these are the kinds of recipes that allow lots of leeway for seasoning to taste. It fits with the notion of finding what your guests are fondest of and having it for them.

When so much is coldly corporate and chrome these days, we need from each other all the little touches that say, "This is a special occasion; you are a special person; you are worth extra attention in my home." Our immediate and extended families are shrinking and geographically frag-

mented; old friends often live far away. Why should country inns be the only substitutes?

2

Special
Occasions
and
Menus

DINNERS

Of all the possible forms of entertaining, small dinners are my favorite. As a friend of mine once said, "Something special happens when people eat together." And, it seems to me, it happens most reliably in the context of an evening meal with a small group. The promise of good food to come and, later, the glow of having been well fed, mellows almost everyone.

I think six is the ideal number for a dinner party. A group of four people puts a little pressure on everybody to keep conversation going, and with eight you feel that you have almost too many people for everyone to get a good conversational turn. But with six at the table the conversation can drift comfortably to include the entire table, to break occasionally in pairs or threesomes, and nobody has to work overly hard at making it happen.

Most contemporary recipes, including those in this book, are for six portions. Don't worry, though, if you want to serve eight; my portions are plenty generous enough to stretch, without having to calculate increases in ingredients. And if you want to serve four, you can count on having a full meal in leftovers.

The menus and recipes in this section are oriented to your doing much of the preparation ahead of time, a technique that lets you lead the way in creating that mellow atmosphere among your guests.

AN ELEGANT DINNER
Serves 6

Mint Juleps
Pineapple–Mint Fizz

Salmon Pâté
Marinated Mushrooms
Whole Wheat Dill Crisps

English Pea Soup
Braised Quail on Rice
Sautéed Spinach
Gold Medallion Carrots
Cucumber and Onion Marinade

Sourdough Biscuits

Cheesecake with Raspberry–Orange Sauce

Preparation and Serving

- Everything may be prepared ahead except the rice, sourdough biscuits, and sautéed spinach; the salmon pâté, marinated mushrooms, and dilled wheat crisps may be made as much as a week before using.
- Cook the English pea soup a day or two ahead.
- Cook the braised quail and gold medallion carrots earlier the same day as dinner to reheat at serving time.
- Begin steaming rice shortly after guests begin to arrive. Offer the pâté, mushrooms and wheat thins with drinks in the living room.
- Have everything assembled to mix the biscuits so that you can shape them and put them into the oven as guests are sitting down to soup. If you are serving the pea soup cold, place a bowlful at each diner's place before the guests come to the table. To serve it hot, ladle from a tureen and pass the bowls after all are seated.
- The cucumbers should be at each place in individual dishes when guests sit down.
- Have the spinach cleaned, dried and ready to sauté quickly in the pan as you are arranging the quail over the rice. Mound the cooked carrots in the center of a shallow serving bowl and make a ring around them with the sautéed spinach.

- To serve the entrée, present the platter of quail and rice to the host or a chosen guest to serve, passing plates for each diner. Then pass the vegetable bowl for guests to help themselves. Bring in the hot biscuits immediately after serving the quail.
- When guests are done with the main meal, offer a bowlful of warm damp towels (easily heated in the microwave oven). Clear the table and bring in dessert while guests are using the towels. Collect the towels in the same bowl before you sit down to begin dessert.
- To serve the dessert, cut the cheesecake at the table and pass individual servings on dessert plates. Pass the sauce in a pitcher.

Table Decorations

Nothing is more attractive for this meal than single seasonal blooms floating in clear glass bowls or a half-dozen florist's carnations arranged with ferns in a glass or silver pitcher. To make the table appear *really* elegant, tie the pitcher with a lace bow and tie each napkin into a butterfly with small pieces of lace.

A FALL DINNER
Serves 6 to 8

Savannah Punch
Fruit Punch

Salmon Pâté with Whole Wheat Dill Crisps

Peanut Soup
Pork Chops with Yams
Rice-Stuffed Vegetables
Cranberry–Apple Sauce

Herbed Potato Rolls

Fresh Sliced Pineapple
Pumpkin Cookies

Preparation and Serving

You can take care of everything in this menu ahead of time.

- The soup can be served hot or cold.
- The pork chops and vegetables may be assembled ahead and baked just before serving, or they may be baked a day ahead and reheated in the microwave oven.
- Refrigerator dough for the rolls will keep for up to a week before shaping and baking. Pop the shaped and raised rolls into the oven just before guests are due to arrive to fill the house with yeasty aroma. Reheating them will take only a minute or so in the microwave oven.
- The pumpkin cookies will stay fresh in the freezer up to three months. Thaw them while you're setting the table.
- Cover the sliced pineapple with plastic wrap to keep it good in the refrigerator for as long as 24 hours.

Table Decorations

Easy decorations for a fall dinner include bouquets of garden mums, autumn leaves, arrangements of miniature pumpkins and Indian corn, or bowls of apples or grapes flanked with candles.

NEW SOUTH CHICKEN DINNER
Serves 6 to 8

Whiskey Sours
Lemon–Grape Fizz

Spiced Pecans
Homemade Roasted Peanuts

Crab and Mushroom Soup
Suelaine's Oven-Fried Chicken
Orange Rice Pileau
Broccoli Casserole
Pineapple Baked Apples
Cold Vegetable Mélange

Sweet Potato Biscuits

Glazed Sliced Oranges
Mama's Soft Sugar Cookies

Preparation and Serving

This meal can be prepared almost entirely in advance, except for the drinks.

- Store spiced pecans, roasted peanuts, and sugar cookies in the freezer for as much as three weeks.
- Cook the soup earlier in the day but don't add the milk until you reheat the soup in a double boiler at serving time.
- Assemble the oven-fried chicken the day before and refrigerate to bake about an hour before serving.
- The rice, broccoli, and apples are all good cooked a day ahead and reheated.
- The cold vegetable mélange will keep, covered, in the refrigerator for two or three days, as will the glazed sliced oranges.
- Assemble the ingredients for the sweet potato biscuits, keeping liquids and dry ingredients separate, to mix, shape, and bake just before dinner.

Table Decorations

For humorous table decorations, ask for a couple of clean boxes from your local Kentucky Fried Chicken franchise and use them as holders for several small pots of philodendron. For a more genteel statement, use wicker baskets to hold the plants and flank them with candles in wooden or clay candlesticks.

DINNER FOR NEW YEAR'S DAY
For a Few or a Crowd

Champagne Coolers
Grapefruit Spritzers

Crabmeat Mold
Benne (Sesame) Seed Crackers

Cold Fruit Soup
Chicken with Black-eyed Peas (with steamed rice)
Endive Salad with Bacon Dressing

White Cornmeal Muffins

Apples & Oranges Frozen Whip

Preparation and Serving

- Only the muffins and salad require last-minute attention.
- Make the crabmeat mold and cold fruit soup a day or two ahead and refrigerate them.
- The chicken can be prepared the day before and reheated, or you can prepare the individual elements of the dish and have the casserole baking in the oven when guests arrive.
- Set the rice to steam as guests are beginning to arrive.
- Have the endive ready and the bacon dressing in the pan so that all you have to do is heat it and mix the salad.
- Similarly, have everything ready for the muffins so that you need only stir the ingredients together, pour the batter into muffin cups, and bake while guests are enjoying drinks.
- Remove the frozen whip from the freezer about halfway through the meal.

Table Decorations

Fill a pretty silver bowl with noisemakers, champagne corks, and white carnations. An easier, less expensive decoration may be made by filling several nice glass containers to different levels with dried black-eyed peas, raw rice, and a small bunch of clean, dry collards.

SUPPER AT THE BEACH HOUSE
For a Few or a Crowd

Beer or Lemonade in Frosted Mugs

Potted Shrimp (with sesame crackers)

Clam Stew
Lettuce with Cucumber and Onion Marinade

Crusty Wheat Bread

Southern Banana Cake
Watermelon with Wine Jelly

Preparation and Serving

This is a truly carefree menu.

- Everything can be cooked ahead, so that all you have to do is come in from the beach or the boat, remove the potted shrimp, cucumbers, lettuce, and watermelon from the refrigerator, take the bread and cake from the freezer, and turn on the heat under the clam stew.
- If you leave the stew in a slow cooker and get out the bread and cake before you leave the house, you won't even have to do that.
- You might want to take a minute to warm the bread in the microwave oven, but it isn't necessary, especially in summer.

Table Decorations

The obvious decorations for this celebration are a few perfect seashells arranged on clean sand in a shallow pottery bowl, or a row of small folded paper boats personalized with the names of your guests "sailing" the length of the table.

GLORIOUS
SOUTHERN
BREAKFASTS

*At breakfast, coffee and cream like liquid gold; six kinds of
bread, each* hot, *as bread always is in the South, and all delicious with butter rich as honey; amber-colored honey also,
with a fragrance as if gathered from the flowers that bloom on
Hymettus! The steaks, so juicy and flavorable; broiled chickens
just delicately crisped and more delicately buttered; fresh fish
from a pond, nicely browned to a turn; ham the tint of a blood
peach; and I know not what other delicacies. [A Virginia breakfast described by a visitor, Kate Conyngham, in 1860, in* The
Sunny South or the Southerner at Home.]

Visitors describing breakfast in the South inevitably comment on two
features, the huge assortment of foods, and the hot breads. In reading the old accounts, you'll be struck by the number of foods they
ate for breakfast that we no longer treat as traditional breakfast fare. Kate
Conyngham mentions succotash and hominy; Harriet Martineau even ate
radishes.

Neither your time schedule nor your pocketbook nor your cholesterol
count allow such breakfasts today, but it's easier than you'd think to duplicate the sense of a groaning board at breakfast just by serving up a couple
of hot breads and an item or two, such as a vegetable or cooked fruit, that
are outside our usual eggs–grits–ham routine. The following menus offer
suggestions for striking a balance between comfortably familiar and
appealingly novel breakfasts. Don't hesitate to add anything else that
appeals to you to the menus. If it tastes good, guests will like it; if it's
unusual, they'll remember it; if they hate it, they'll eat something else.

It's especially important at breakfasts and brunches to serve foods that
don't require your constant attention. For instance, try the recipe for an
oven pancake that is baked and cut into several servings instead of trying
to flip pancakes for everyone, or try the apple pancake you can freeze and
reheat instead of doing any last-minute mixing at all. Serve baked or
scrambled eggs that can be done all in a batch to get out of the over-easy-a-
dozen-times trap. And instead of trying to make two slices of toast at a
time and keep it hot, serve hot biscuits, rolls, and muffins. After all, that's
what the South is famous for.

AN ELEGANT BREAKFAST
Serves 6

Honeydew Melon with Cranberry Jelly
Foolproof Cheese Soufflé
Garden Relish
Blueberry–Bran Muffins
Sweet Potato Biscuits

A HEARTY BREAKFAST
Serves 6 to 8

Ambrosia
Roast Beef Hash (with Eggs)
Cucumber and Onion Marinade
Golden Cheese Grits
Georgia Riz Biscuits (with Honey)

A LIGHT BREAKFAST
Serves 4 to 6

Iced Raspberries or Cherries
Oven Pancake with Brandied Peaches
Cranberry–Apple Sauce

A CONTINENTAL BREAKFAST
Serves 2 to 20

Grapefruit Spritzers
Fresh Fruit Skewers
Sliced Swiss Cheese
Hard Boiled Eggs
Sally Lunn Buns
Hemlock Inn's Bran Muffins
Crisp Biscuits

A BREAKFAST BUFFET
For a Crowd

Karen's Breakfast Scramble
Fruit Skewers
Brandied Peaches
Ambrosia
Sweet Potatoes in Orange Shells
Eggplant in Tomato Sauce
Sourdough Biscuits
Cornmeal Muffins
Whole Wheat Bread

TWO MISSED-BREAKFAST SNACKS

Tomato Juice
Baked Bananas with Strawberries Flambé
Old-Time Bran Muffins
Fruit in Season
Apple Pancake
Homemade Vanilla Ice Cream

A
POTPOURRI
OF
PARTIES

AN IMPROMPTU REPAST

Cold Sliced Smoked Turkey or Baked Ham
Orange Rice Pileau
Cold Vegetable Mélange
Homemade Ice Cream
Pumpkin Cookies

A passion for a party means having one any time the opportunity arises. The neighbors buy a new ice-cream freezer, a date turns out especially well, a friend drops in unexpectedly, your kid gets a job and brings home a first paycheck and three new friends—*anything nice* offers an excuse for an impromptu repast. The only preparation it requires is having taken the trouble to stock the sorts of food you can whip out and fancy up slightly at a moment's notice.

In truth, some of the impromptu repasts I remember most fondly didn't involve even that much advance preparation. During my years in graduate school, I traveled with several colleagues almost every weekend to teach communications workshops. We'd travel Friday afternoon, teach all day Saturday, and drag home that night. One of our number pointed out that we weren't having much fun and that our Friday evening meals in restaurants were getting repetitious.

We decided to break the monotony by having a dinner party in our hotel room. As usual, none of us had any money, so we planned a "stone fondu" party. Our most reliable member volunteered to bring the fondu pot and a bottle of oil. Beyond that, everyone was simply supposed to bring something that seemed likely to do well in a fondu pot. We ordered up a bottle of hotel wine, set up our party on a coffee table and—sitting on the floor—had a giggly and not very professional evening eating bits of meat, mushrooms, cauliflower and chewing on hunks of French bread.

A simpler impromptu repast I remember vividly came during my days as a newspaper editor and writer. A quirk in the advertising schedule cut the size of the paper one day, and another reporter and I found ourselves finished several hours early in a gorgeous spring afternoon.

My colleague ran to the store and picked up a six-pack of dark beer, while I hustled home to grab a loaf of whole-wheat bread and a hunk of strong cheddar cheese. We headed to the fish hatchery, where we sat in the grass next to a row of rectangular ponds full of rainbow trout. We admired their shining beauty, put their unavoidable futures out of our minds, and sitting there in the sun, consumed a most satisfying meal without benefit of any utensil but a sharp knife and bottle opener.

The menu above may be a bit more complicated than that, but even so it is more a strategy than a prescription for particular foods. You shouldn't have trouble finding a little cold sliced meat of some kind. Marinated vegetables keep in the refrigerator, and orange rice is quick and easy to prepare. Homemade ice cream can be made on a whim, or you could substitute very high quality commercial ice cream tucked away in the freezer for special occasions. Pumpkin cookies, like most cookies, freeze beautifully. The possible variations go on and on.

Table Decorations

The fun here should include an impromptu table decoration—a party hat or Mardi Gras beads left over from other celebrations, perhaps, or a fan folded from brown paper and decorated in crayon.

JUST FOR TWO

Champagne or Sparkling Cider
Scallop Salad with Dill–Mustard Dressing
Whole Wheat Dill Crisps
Blackberry–Orange Parfait

In *Raney,* Clyde Edgerton captures the essence of a private special occasion, or at least the beginnings of one, in a passage about the arrangements Charles made for his honeymoon with Raney. Raney tells about it:

> First of all, Charles had rib-eye steaks rolled into our room on this metal table with drawers which could keep the steaks warm. And there in the middle of the table was a dozen red roses. All that was nice.
> But in this silver bucket with ice and a white towel was, of all things, a bottle of champagne.

The fact that the rest of the evening didn't work out as either Charles or Raney had planned doesn't fault the intimate little supper one bit.

This menu duplicates the mood, though it's more practical, as Scallop Salad can be prepared ahead of time. And a single red rose will be every bit as effective as a dozen, and lots more affordable.

Table Decorations

This kind of party beckons for a single flower tied with a tiny bow and two *very* fancy napkins as decorations.

AN AFTERNOON DESSERT PARTY
For a Large Group

> York Gingerbread with Chef's Sweet Whipped Cream
> Aunt Chloe's Charlotte Russe
> The Lightest Cheesecake
> Minted Fresh Apricots
> Iced Cherries
> Coffee (including decaf)
> Tea
> Herb Tea
> Ice Water with Lemon Slices

You hardly need a menu to throw a dessert party—an increasingly popular entertainment option. Any of the recipes from the dessert section of this book will do nicely—and easily. Remember, though, that part of the fun is variety. Offer enough different desserts for each guest to try at least three different ones. Do as Mama did in Ruth Moose's story, "Green Lightning and the Tablecloth Bride," (which is about what has to be one of the most spontaneous parties ever) and cut the pieces smaller. Out of deference to people who need to restrict fat and sugar in their diets, always include at least one very light dessert and a couple of kinds of fruit in your menu.

Table Decorations
I think a light-hearted table decoration goes nicely with the light desserts. Assembling a few raw ingredients, such as chocolate chips, nuts, and grated coconut, in pretty glass containers of various sizes is effective, especially if you have a few antique cookie cutters (or even new ones) to work into the arrangement.

AFTERNOON TEA
For Any Number

> Whole Wheat Bread (thinly sliced)
> Salmon Pâté
> Ambrosia
> Holiday Chocolate Cake
> Spiced Pecans
> Coffee
> Tea
> Herb Tea

Like the British, Southerners in the Old South hung onto the custom of afternoon tea tenaciously. At last the rest of us are beginning to cultivate the custom too. Some teas have been prodigiously heavy, almost full meals, while others have been little more than the tea itself and a simple sweet to go with it. To make it special requires mainly an attractive tea service (this is not the place for styrofoam cups!), some truly tasty tea (it's not the place for Tetley's instant, either) and an agreement among guests and hostess to proceed at reduced pace, talking about pleasant things.

OUTDOOR
PARTIES
AND
PICNICS

Any food becomes special the minute you go outside to eat it. A Southern pig pickin' for a hundred people and a sandwich and apple you eat alone in the woods are equally special because you're eating in an out-of-the-ordinary situation, where all your senses are stimulated by the breezes and brightness. (And Mother Nature takes care of the decorations!)

My earliest memory of eating outside and finding it special goes back to when I was ten or so and dearly loved to spend Saturday mornings in my hemlock hutch in the woods. I would string myself several necklaces of Cheerios, with an occasional marshmallow worked in, and so adorned I would head up the hill to the woods, where I filled a battered tin cup with spring water and settled onto the pine needles under my shelter to sip and nibble as I read Nancy Drew.

That, of course, was a solo mission. Entertaining someone other than yourself out of doors takes a little more planning and preparation. It's important to have a contingency plan. What will you do if weather is bad? Just praying for sunshine isn't enough. For all you know, a truck farmer in the same county may be poking at his corn and praying for an all-day rain, and there's a likelihood that in prayers, produce will win over parties. Better to plan an emergency shelter of some sort. Rent a dining tent or an awning or plan your party for an area that has a picnic pavilion. If you're using your own patio or balcony, work out a way to keep a door open so that food and guests can move inside quickly if rain begins.

Go ahead and pray, but keep the awning handy, too.

A SOPHISTICATED COOKOUT
For Any Number

Beer or Champagne
Old-Fashioned Lemonade
Oysters and Clams on the Grill
Grilled Chicken
Rice Salad
Eggplant in Tomato Sauce
Garden Relish
Refrigerator Potato Bread
Gingerbread Cupcakes
Boiled Coffee

A successful cookout depends on keeping everything as simple as possible and cooking some of the goods ahead of time, inside, leaving only one or two things for ceremonial outdoor grilling. Choose foods that can be carried hot in casseroles and those that are good at room temperature so that you don't have to worry about keeping anything chilled or very hot.

The nice thing about outdoor entertaining is that you can encourage guests to watch the grill and distribute beverages and have them believing that doing it is part of the fun. Also, it's proper to get right to it, no worrying about appetizers and pre-dinner preliminaries.

This kind of entertaining works beautifully not only in your yard or on your patio, but also in public parks and at the private picnic grounds of companies, clubs, and churches. Wherever you do it, be sure to get the fire started a little earlier than seems necessary. It always takes longer than you expect to bring a fire to cooking temperature.

Although our forebears may have carried the ancestral silver and crystal to the picnic site, you'll have more fun if you use unbreakable dinnerware.

THE ULTIMATE PICNIC
Serves 4 to 6

Chilled White Wine
Old-Fashioned Limeade
Potted Shrimp (with Melba Toast)
Indoor Smoked Turkey
Whole Wheat Bread
Fresh Fruit Skewers
Southern Banana Cupcakes

A picnic is a portable party. Anything you can carry, you can serve outside. The setting and the escape from ordinary routine matter most. Here are two examples.

Once my husband and I went with older friends to a state park for Sunday morning breakfast. Shortly after dawn, fortified only with coffee, we bounced along the mountain roads conversing perfunctorily. When we got to the park, after Frank started the fire, Marty got a pot of coffee perking and began to fry bacon in a huge skillet. We sat around the fire waiting and talking, sipping coffee and enjoying the mingling aromas of bacon and spring foliage.

When the bacon was crisp, Marty drained it on a newspaper, poured most of the fat into the fire, and broke a dozen eggs into the pan.

As I remember it, that was all we had, bacon, eggs, and coffee. Simple. No fuss, no hassle.

With the food in our bellies, we began to get lively. Frank started quoting from *Hiawatha*, until he ran out of verses he knew, then he started making them up, improvising on the theme of wild strawberries. This led us to take a walk in the woods looking for wild strawberries. Since it was September, we found none, but I don't recall that we were particularly disappointed.

After the walk, we finished the coffee and packed up the skillet. Frank was still declaiming as we climbed back into the car giggling. It was barely noon. We laughed and invented poetry all the way back to town, high on our own hilarity.

The second ultimate picnic was a gourmet's delight, complicated in its offerings but simple in final execution. We went with our friends George and Marie to a lakeside picnic spot. They brought a couple of bottles of good white wine, better than any of us could really afford at the time, which we chilled in the creek. Marie had made a loaf of sweet, dark, spicy bread—definitely not our daily bread—that was delicious cold. We also had eggs deviled with capers, packed for carrying in an egg carton lined with watercress. I remember a lot of sliced rare roast beef, fresh scallions, and a loaf of French bread that had been hollowed out, filled with shrimp salad and refrigerated overnight.

For dessert we had oranges, apples, and chunks of chocolate fudge. And the rest of the wine.

The eating and drinking took a long time. When we were done we didn't talk about poetry or art or much of anything. We took a half-hearted walk along the shore and finally gave up and took a nap in the sun.

In planning your own ultimate picnic, pick a spot that is special to you for some reason and do whatever it takes to make the whole event different from your daily life. If you usually take your children, leave them at home; if you usually leave them, take them along. Instead of going with the people who you entertain all the time, invite someone you like but rarely see. Go early in the morning or late in the evening. Serve foods either more simple or more elaborate than you usually take on picnics. And go for fun.

3

Recipes

BREAKFAST, BRUNCH, AND LUNCH

Oven Pancakes

For a heartier breakfast, you can fill the pancakes with cold fruit, sautéed apples, or warm Brandied Peaches (p. 119)—or serve with berries and whipped cream.

To adjust the recipe according to the crowd, simply figure 1 egg, 1/4 cup flour, and 1/4 cup milk for each person and use larger or smaller skillets as necessary. The size doesn't have to be exact, as long as the batter fills each skillet by about half. Don't worry if you make extra. Someone will eat it.

> 6 eggs
> 1 1/2 cups flour
> 1 1/2 cups milk
> 1 teaspoon salt
> 1 teaspoon vanilla (optional)
> 4 tablespoons butter
> Ground nutmeg
> Powdered sugar

Preheat oven to 450°.

Place all ingredients except the butter and nutmeg in the work jar of a blender or food processor and process until smooth.

On top of the stove, melt 2 tablespoons butter in each of 2 cast-iron 10- or 12-inch skillets. The skillets should be hot, but not so that the butter burns. Divide the batter between the two skillets and place them immediately in the preheated oven. Bake at 450° for 15 minutes, then lower heat to 350° and bake 10–15 minutes longer, until the pancakes are puffed and brown.

To prepare ahead, make the batter the night before and refrigerate. Stir or process briefly before pouring into the heated skillet. Also, prepare the filling and refrigerate either for reheating or serving cold.

To serve, either bring the skillets directly to the table or transfer the pancakes to two serving dishes. Dust the pancakes with powdered sugar and serve.

Makes 6 servings.

Apple Pancake

You can whip up this pancake in no time with a blender or food processor. The first time I made it everyone in my family stood around the kitchen sampling and making suggestions for toppings. We had votes for maple syrup, whipped cream, cold applesauce, and light molasses. I chose vanilla ice cream. Then we tried it in soup bowls with cold milk poured over it. My sainted magnolias, but it's good all those ways!

> 2–3 apples
> 1/4 cup butter
> Ground cinnamon
> 2 eggs, beaten
> 1 1/3 cups milk
> 3 tablespoons granulated sugar
> 1/2 teaspoon vanilla extract
> 2 cups self-rising flour
> Ground nutmeg (optional)

Preheat oven to 450°.

Peel, core, and slice the apples. Melt the butter in a 10- or 12-inch iron skillet, swirling it around so the sides are completely coated. Cover the bottom of the pan with the apples. Sprinkle them heavily with cinnamon.

In the blender or food processor, blend the eggs, milk, sugar, and vanilla. Add the flour and blend again until the mixture is smooth. Pour the batter over the apples. Grate a small amount of nutmeg over the batter if you wish.

Bake 15–20 minutes, until the batter is cooked through and the pancake begins to come away from the sides of the pan. Turn the pancake out onto a serving plate carefully, using a spatula to coax all the apples loose from the bottom of the pan if necessary. Serve hot with any topping that appeals to you. May be baked ahead and reheated in the microwave oven.

Makes 6 servings.

Foolproof Cheese Soufflé

Use the best bread you can find to make this soufflé. I recommend Refrigerator Potato Bread (p. 140). It's fine if it is slightly stale. Some people cut off the crusts for appearance's sake, but I think it's silly.

> 9 slices bread, cubed
> 1 pound Gouda or Edam cheese, grated
> 3 eggs
> 3 cups milk
> 1 teaspoon dry mustard
> Salt and pepper

Arrange layers of bread and cheese in a greased 2-quart baking dish. Beat or process in the blender the eggs, milk, mustard, and salt and pepper to taste. Pour over the bread and cheese. *Refrigerate at least 8 hours, or up to 24 hours.*

To cook, bake 1 hour in a 325° oven, or until puffed and set in the center. If you use a glass baking dish, put the soufflé into a cold oven and then turn the heat to 325° so an abrupt temperature change won't break the glass.

Makes 6–8 servings.

> *Variations*
> - Substitute Whole Wheat Bread (page 00) for white bread.
> - Substitute Swiss or Cheddar cheese for Edam or Gouda.
> - Add crumbled cooked bacon, chopped cooked ham, or crabmeat to the cheese.
> - Beat 1/4 cup finely chopped parsley with the milk and eggs.

Roast Beef Hash

Obviously the measurements don't have to be exact to make a good hash.
The recipe is infinitely expandable.

2 tablespoons butter
2 tablespoons oil
1 onion, chopped
1 green pepper
4 large baking potatoes, peeled and chopped
2 cups chopped roast beef
Stock or water to moisten
Salt and pepper
Dried vegetable flake seasoning
Dried red pepper
6 fresh eggs (optional)

Melt butter and oil in a large cast-iron skillet. Sauté the onion and green
pepper until soft but not brown. Add the potatoes and beef, and stir to
blend in the sautéed vegetables.

*To prepare ahead, roast the beef and bake the potatoes earlier in the week. As
much as a day before serving, assemble the ingredients as directed and refrigerate
until ready to use.*

Cook, uncovered, over medium heat until the bottom is brown. Do not
stir or turn too soon or the hash will stick. Once the bottom has browned,
turn the hash to cook the other side. Don't worry about keeping it unbro-
ken. Add stock or water if the hash seems too dry. Season to taste.

To serve with eggs, make indentations in the hot hash, break in eggs,
add a little stock or water to make steam, cover the pan and cook over
medium heat until the eggs are set—3–5 minutes. To use the microwave,
cook the hash according to the directions above as much as a day before
serving. At serving time, arrange the hash on a microwave safe serving
dish, break the eggs into indentations, cover loosely with plastic wrap and
microwave 3–6 minutes, until hash is hot and eggs are set.

Makes 6 servings.

Variations

- Substitute corned beef, ham, or
  chopped clams for roast beef.
- Add chopped parsley and celery leaves
  when you sauté the onion and pepper.
- Add chopped beets along with the
  potato.
- Melt grated cheese on top of the hash,
  with or without eggs.

Karen's Breakfast Scramble

This is one of the easiest and tastiest buffet dishes I know of. Make a little more than you think you'll need because people always come back for more. For each diner, allow:

> Butter
> 1 medium-sized red boiled potato, skin on, sliced
> 1/2 medium onion, sliced
> 1/4 cup chopped cooked ham or corned beef
> 1 egg, beaten
> 1/4 cup cottage cheese
> 2 tablespoons dry Pepperidge Farm Poultry Stuffing
> Salt and pepper
> Sliced tomatoes or oranges

In a heavy skillet melt enough butter to cover the bottom of the pan generously. Over medium heat, sauté the potato and onion until the onion begins to soften. Stir in the cooked meat. When all these ingredients are hot, pour in the beaten egg and cook until the egg is barely set. Remove from the heat. The egg will continue to cook for several minutes. Stir in the cottage cheese and dry stuffing, and salt and pepper to taste. Move the scrambled eggs to a warm platter and season to taste. Garnish with tomatoes, or oranges if tomatoes are out of season. For buffet service, use an electric warming tray.

To prepare ahead, have all ingredients ready and refrigerated so that all you have to do is scramble them together to serve.

Makes 1 serving. Multiply ingredients for each additional diner.

DINNER
ENTRÉES

Baked Ham

Curing techniques were matters of personal pride, with
each farmer or planter adding his own flourishes to the
basic technique. Pepper, alum, ashes, charcoal, corn meal,
honey, sugar, molasses, saltpeter, mustard, and a host of
other seasonings were added, and each producer fancied
his own meat to be "not inferior to the best Wesphalian
hams."
—Sam Bowers Hilliard, *Hog Meat and Hoecake*

Ham is excellent for entertaining because almost everybody likes it. The
common lament is that you can't buy authentic country ham or sweet ham
as it used to be. (A country ham is older, drier, and saltier than a sweet
ham.) The truth is, unless you know a farmer who produces his own, you
cannot. But the ham that *is* available can taste fine.

Ask any man and he'll tell you that, for true Southern eating, the only
acceptable thing to do with a country ham is to cut slices from it, fry them in
a hot skillet, and make red-eye gravy by pouring in a little water or coffee
and boiling it up to de-glaze the pan. Pour the resulting broth over the ham
on the plate, he'll say. Sop it up with biscuits.

However, the cookbook-approved version (circulated mostly by ladies)
of preparing country ham instructs you to pare off the mold, scrub the ham
with a brush, soak it overnight in cold water, boil it in anything from cider to
Coke or beer, skin it, glaze it, and bake it.

With a sweet ham you can skip the scrubbing, soaking and boiling, and
go directly from skinning to baking.

With a boneless, pre-cooked ham you can simply put it in the oven and
heat it through by baking at 350° for about 20 minutes a pound.

And when you're really pressed, you can go to a good supermarket or
delicatessen and order a ham to be cooked and sliced for the day you want
to pick it up. It won't taste like Ne-maw May's home cured, mustard-and-
molasses-glazed Thanksgiving ham, but there's no use in trying to be perfect in an imperfect world.

Low-Country Chicken and Shrimp Bog

This great make-ahead dish tastes so good people remember it from one time to the next. Plan to cook it in a pan from which it can also be served.

12–14 chicken drumsticks
1 pound smoked sausage
1 celery rib, chopped
1 large onion, chopped
1 large leek, chopped
1/2 pound mushrooms, sliced
1/4 cup chopped parsley
2 cups raw brown rice
31/2 cups stock
1 bay leaf
1 pound shrimp
1 10-ounce package frozen baby peas
4 ounces pimento

Brown the chicken in a large skillet. An electric skillet is excellent for cooking and serving. Remove the chicken from the pan and set aside. Cut the sausage into bite-size pieces and brown. Remove the sausage from the pan and set aside. Pour excess fat out of the pan. In the same pan, over medium heat, sauté the celery, onion, leek, mushrooms, and parsley until soft. Add the rice. Cook and stir until all the grains are coated with fat and the rice begins to look translucent.

Pour in the stock. Add the bay leaf. Arrange the chicken pieces on top of the rice. Put the sausage between the pieces of chicken. Bring to a boil, cover the pan, reduce heat, and simmer until the rice is tender—40–50 minutes. Add extra stock or water if mixture becomes too dry. *The recipe may be prepared as much as a day ahead to this point.*

To serve, arrange the shrimp (shelled or not, depending on the formality of the occasion) in a border around the edges of the pan. Make a second border, inside the shrimp, with the frozen peas. Arrange the pimento attractively across the peas. Raise the heat, cover the pan, and steam just until the shrimp are done and the peas are hot—about 5–10 minutes. Do not overcook.

Serve directly from the pan.

Makes 8 servings, though I've seen 6 people eat it all.

Chicken with Black-eyed Peas

The first time I tasted this I couldn't believe such simple ingredients could produce a dish so delicious. I cannot imagine anyone not liking it. Allow at least two pieces of chicken for each diner. Except for the black-eyes, the recipe is easily cooked all in one skillet. The electric skillet is ideal for preparing and serving this dish.

> 1 pound dried black-eyed peas
> 12 or more chicken thighs and drumsticks
> 2 eggs, beaten
> 2 cups flour
> 1 tablespoon poultry seasoning
> 1/4 cup oil
> 2 tablespoons butter
> 1 medium onion, chopped
> 1/2 pound fresh mushrooms, sliced
> 1 garlic clove, peeled and mashed
> 1 cup chopped canned tomatoes
> 1 cup dry white wine
> Salt to taste

Soak the peas overnight, then simmer until tender. This may be done several days before you prepare the rest of the recipe.

Rinse and dry the chicken. Dip each piece in the beaten egg to coat.

Shake the chicken pieces in a large plastic bag with the flour and poultry seasoning.

Heat the oil and butter together in a large skillet and brown the chicken pieces in it. Drain the chicken on paper towels. Pour out any remaining fat.

Sauté the onion in the same skillet until the onion is translucent. Set the onions aside.

On high heat, sauté the mushrooms rapidly just until they begin to darken around the edges. Set the mushrooms aside.

Drain the blackeyes and canned tomatoes, reserving liquid from both. Put the beans into the skillet. Mix in the sautéed onion and the garlic clove.

Arrange the chicken pieces on top of the beans. Scatter the mushrooms and tomatoes between the chicken pieces.

Salt to taste.

Pour in just enough wine to show through the beans.

Cover and simmer 20–30 minutes, adding more wine, bean liquid or tomato juice as needed.

This recipe can be prepared ahead and reheated. It will look prettier if you prepare, hold, reheat, and serve it all in the same skillet.

Makes 6 servings.

Braised Quail on Rice

If there are no hunters in your family you can still enjoy quail. They're now raised domestically and sold in the grocery store, where you can buy them frozen. If you don't find them in the freezer ask that they be ordered for you.

Allow two quail for each serving with a few extras for big eaters. *Cornish hen halves may be substituted for the quail, 1 hen half for 2 quail, in this recipe.*

12 quail
2 tablespoons butter
2 tablespoons oil
1/3 cup dry white wine
Salt to taste
1/4 cup chopped celery leaves
1/4 cup chopped fresh parsley
3 cups cooked white rice
1/4 cup chopped fresh chives or green onion tops
Lemon juice

Thaw, wash and dry the quail.

Heat the butter and oil in a heavy skillet and brown the quail lightly. Add the wine and salt to taste. Reduce heat to low, cover the pan tightly, and steam gently for about 30 minutes, adding more wine if necessary.

At the end of 30 minutes, add celery leaves and parsley and steam for 15–20 minutes more, adding more liquid if the quail seem dry. Steam until the legs move easily in the sockets. *Quail may be prepared in advance to this point.*

Just before serving, bring the pan juices to a quick boil. Lower heat and simmer to heat the quail through.

Arrange quail on top of cooked white rice on a warm serving platter. Pour pan juices over them, sprinkle with chopped chives, and squeeze lemon juice over all.

To heat pre-prepared quail in the microwave, prepare the serving platter completely, with the rice and fowl, reserving the juices. At serving time, cover loosely with plastic wrap and reheat about 10 minutes, more or less depending on your microwave. Remove from the oven. Heat the reserved pan juices in a cup for about 1 minute. Pour over quail and rice. Sprinkle with chopped chives and lemon juice.

Makes 6 servings.

> ▪ Quail traditionally are eaten with the fingers. When everyone is about done, it's a thoughtful touch to pass around warm damp cloths that have been perfumed with a touch of lemon extract.

Suelaine's Oven-Fried Chicken

Well, of course it isn't *real* old-fashioned fried chicken—done in a deep skillet with lard, then drained to make cream gravy with the drippings—but it is very good, hot or cold. And like old-style fried chicken, it is crispy on the outside, with the juices sealed inside. Before I tried it, I was skeptical about using buttermilk to bind the coating, but it works perfectly, eliminating the need for egg, and doesn't taste the least bit buttermilky.

> 6 chicken quarters
> 1 cup buttermilk
> 3 heaping cups cornflakes
> 1/4 cup dried parsley
> 1 teaspoon poultry seasoning
> 1/2 teaspoon cayenne pepper

Preheat oven to 350°.

Dip the chicken quarters into the buttermilk and set aside.

Crush the cornflakes, but not too fine—a few coarse pieces add crispness.

Mix the seasonings into the cornflakes, then roll each piece of chicken in the mixture to coat.

Arrange the chicken pieces in a flat baking pan so that the pieces don't touch each other. *The chicken may be prepared ahead to this point and refrigerated.*

Bake for 1 hour.

Makes 6 generous servings.

Indoor Smoked Turkey

If you're a purist, this won't sound good to you; at first, it didn't to me, either. I was surprised to discover that even if it doesn't have an old-time smokehouse flavor, it is very good, especially for a picnic or outdoor meal.

> 2 quarts water
> 1 bottle (3½ ounces) Hickory brand liquid smoke
> 1 small turkey or turkey breast

Preheat oven to 350°.

Make a marinade by combining the water and liquid smoke. Place the turkey in a large plastic bag, pour in the marinade, seal, and refrigerate for 12–24 hours. (The longer it marinates, the smokier the flavor will be.) Move the turkey around in the bag a few times to make sure the marinade reaches all parts equally.

Remove the turkey from the marinade. Dry with a paper towel, rub oil over the skin, and roast uncovered for 2½–3½ hours, according to the timing instructions on the turkey label. Cool and refrigerate before serving. *This recipe may be prepared several days ahead of time.*

Serve cold, thinly sliced.

Pork Chops with Yams

4 large yams or sweet potatoes
1 large orange
3/4 cup brown sugar
6 pork chops, about 1 inch thick
Salt and pepper to taste
3 tablespoons water

Preheat oven to 350°.

Cook the yams until just tender by boiling, baking or microwaving. Cook, skin, and cut them into half-inch slices. Thinly slice the orange; remove the seeds but leave on the peel. Arrange layers of yams and orange slices in a greased baking dish, sprinkling each layer with brown sugar. Brown the pork chops in a skillet and season with salt and pepper. Lay the chops over the yams. Pour on 3 tablespoons water. *The dish may be prepared ahead to this point.*

Cover and bake in a 350° oven, about 1 hour, basting occasionally with the syrup in the dish.

Makes 6 servings.

Grilled Chicken

The only thing that takes any effort at all in this recipe is mixing the marinade. Of course starting the charcoal and cooking the chicken require attention—but that's supposed to be part of the fun.

The marinade does not contain salt because the chicken stays juicier without it; there's no sugar because sugar makes the skin burn before the center is done. Multiply the marinade ingredients, if necessary, to have enough to coat all the chicken pieces.

1 cup red wine vinegar
1 cup salad oil
1 tablespoon dried tarragon
1 tablespoon dried basil
1 garlic clove
6 half-chickens or 6 legs and thighs

Combine vinegar, oil and spices to make marinade. Marinate the chicken for 6–24 hours.

Broil over hot charcoal. Do not begin cooking until the coals are white all over. Put the chicken on the grill, bony side down. Cook until the meat is almost done, about 20 minutes, before turning to cook the skin side. Baste often with marinade.

Makes 6 servings.

Charcoal Barbecued Chicken

I absolutely do not want to get into the barbecue wars, so if your idea of barbecued chicken is much different from mine, call this recipe something else. But do try it. Its simplicity is deceptive; it's about the best chicken I've tasted. Also, it has the advantage of cooking more quickly on the grill because of the parboiling step.

> 6 half-chickens or 6 legs and thighs
> 1 cup melted butter
> 1/2 cup cider vinegar
> Cayenne pepper to taste

Steam the chicken in a small amount of water for about 15 minutes. It should be almost, but not quite, done. *This may be refrigerated for as much as 24 hours.*

Combine butter, vinegar and pepper to make sauce. Cook chicken over hot charcoal, brushing frequently with the sauce.

Makes 6 servings.

Oysters and Clams on the Grill

Here's an easy way to enjoy the mystique of an outdoor clam bake or oyster roast without digging holes, soaking burlap, and spreading seaweed.

Scrub clams and oysters and keep them on ice until you are ready to cook them. *This may be done as much as 24 hours ahead.* If the clams are especially sandy, soak them in cold water and cornmeal for an hour or two to get them to spit out the sand.

Fire up the charcoal grill as usual. When all the coals are white, put the clams or oysters on the grate in a single layer. Close the lid, if your grill has one, or cover the clams and oysters with a layer of heavy duty aluminum foil. They are done as soon as the shells begin to open, usually in about 10 minutes. Do not overcook. Use asbestos mittens and tongs to remove the clams and oysters to serving trays.

I won't give quantities here because as far as I've seen, there is no limit to the number of clams or oysters any live human being can eat.

Scallop Salad with Dill–Mustard Dressing

3/4 pound fresh sea scallops
Dried dill weed
2 tablespoons white vinegar
1 egg
1/4 teaspoon dry mustard
1/2 teaspoon salt
1/4 cup olive oil
1/2 cup vegetable oil
Sweet hot prepared mustard
1/2 cup raw frozen green peas
4 green onions, chopped
Boston or Butterhead lettuce

Steam the scallops over (not in) boiling water in a steamer basket until they are just done through. Sprinkle them heavily with dried dill weed. Refrigerate immediately for at least 2 hours or as long as 24 hours.

To make the dressing, combine vinegar, egg, dry mustard, and salt in a blender or food processor. Pulse briefly to mix. Then, with the machine running on high, gradually pour in the oils in a thin stream. The mixture will thicken as it processes. Refrigerate until serving time.

To serve the salad, begin with about 1/4 cup of the refrigerated dressing, combining with the prepared mustard until you have a degree of piquancy you like. (Cover the unused portion of the dressing tightly. It will keep at least a week in the refrigerator and makes an excellent sauce for hot green vegetables.)

Lightly mix the scallops, peas, green onions, and dressing. Pile the salad onto a bed of lettuce to serve. Garnish with sprigs of fresh dill if you can find it.

Makes 2 generous servings.

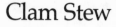

Clam Stew

1/2 pound large white dry limas
1 cup cooked or canned pinto beans
6 slices bacon
2 tablespoons olive oil
1 large onion, chopped
1/2 red bell pepper, chopped
1/2 green bell pepper, chopped
1 rib celery, chopped
1 clove garlic, peeled
2 dozen fresh clams, cooked and scrubbed
  or 4 7-ounce cans chopped clams
Water
Pepper

Cover the limas with cold water and bring to a boil. Cover, lower heat and simmer until the limas are almost falling apart, usually about 2 hours, depending on how dry the beans are. *This can be done several days ahead if you keep the cooked beans refrigerated.*

Mix the pintos and limas in a large soup pan.

In a heavy skillet, fry the bacon slices and drain off the fat. Crumble the bacon, and add it to the beans.

In the same skillet, heat the olive oil and sauté the chopped onion, peppers, celery, and garlic. The vegetables should be soft but not brown. Add them to the beans.

Steam the clams just until they open. Cool, reserving the broth, and chop the clams. If they are very large you may need to rinse out the intestinal matter. Add the chopped clams (or canned clams and canning liquid) to the beans. If you have used fresh clams, add some of the steaming liquid to the beans, tasting as you go so the mixture doesn't get too salty. Add water as needed to get a soupy consistency that suits you, then simmer the mixture together for about 20 minutes, just long enough to blend the flavors. *This may be refrigerated as much as a day ahead of time and reheated for serving.*

Season to taste with ground pepper. No salt should be necessary.

Makes 6 servings.

APPETIZERS

Crabmeat Mold

I've been making this for more than a decade. No one ever seems to get tired of it. I like it best made with good fresh crabmeat, but it's also tasty made with frozen snow crab (which has the advantages of not having to be picked over to remove shell), and with the less expensive imitation crab available at most seafood counters and in some freezer cases.

The original recipe used cream cheese and mayonnaise. I've changed it to the lower-fat Neufchâtel cheese and light salad dressing, with no noticeable change in flavor. Using canned soup in the mold embarrasses me, but I've never found another ingredient that works better in this recipe.

> 1½ cups crabmeat (canned, fresh or frozen)
> ½ can cream of mushroom soup
> 8 ounces Neufchâtel cheese
> 1 envelope plain gelatin
> 2 tablespoons cold water
> 2 tablespoons minced onion
> ½ cup light salad dressing
> ½ cup chopped celery

Pick over the crabmeat, if necessary, to get rid of the shell bits.

In a small saucepan put the soup and cheese, stirring over medium heat until they are mixed.

Soften the gelatin in 2 tablespoons cold water. Mix the gelatin, onion, dressing, celery, and crabmeat into the soup and cheese mixture. Pour into an oiled mold. Chill until set, at least 4 hours.

To serve, unmold on a bed of endive lettuce and serve with crackers. Makes about 3½ cups of spread.

Salmon Pâté

Covered tightly, this pâté will keep at least a week in the refrigerator.

> 1 8-ounce can salmon
> 1 8-ounce package Neufchâtel cheese
> 1 tablespoon lemon juice
> 1 tablespoon horseradish
> 2 tablespoons minced onion
> Liquid smoke (a few drops to taste)
> Coarse salt
> Coarsely ground pepper
> 1/2 lemon, thinly sliced

Drain the salmon. Remove the skin and heaviest bones. Put the salmon into the food processor or blender.

Break the cheese into lumps and add to the salmon. Add all remaining ingredients (except lemon) and process until smooth. Taste and add more liquid smoke if you wish.

Pack the pâté into small crocks or pottery serving bowls. Sprinkle the top lightly with salt and pepper.

Garnish with thin lemon slices. Cover and chill until serving time. Serve with Whole Wheat Dill Crisps (below).

Makes about 2 cups.

Whole Wheat Dill Crisps

Slice stale Whole Wheat Bread (p. 139) into 1/2-inch slices. Spread lightly with butter or margarine. Sprinkle with dried dill weed. Arrange on a cookie sheet. Bake in a 200° oven 1–2 hours, or until crisp but not brown. Cool. *These will keep in a tightly covered tin up to a week.*

Potted Shrimp

Potted Shrimp will keep for a week. It's best made with fresh shrimp, but when you're in a hurry and can't spend time shelling shrimp, frozen peeled shrimp will do. I used to follow the steps listed below for mixing this, but now I just throw it all in the food processor and give it a whirl. If you do it that way be careful not to blend the shrimp so long it turns into mush. That would be expensive baby food.

> 1/2 cup butter
> 1/2 pound cooked shrimp
> 1 clove garlic, minced
> 1 tablespoon chopped fresh parsley
> 1 teaspoon dried dill weed
> 1 teaspoon grated lemon rind
> Cayenne pepper to taste
> Salt to taste

Cream the butter until it is soft. Chop the shrimp and work it in. Mix in all the remaining ingredients, tasting to see if you need more lemon or dill. Pack into a small crock or serving bowl and chill at least overnight (although 2 days is better).

At serving time, bring the spread to cool room temperature. Serve with Whole Wheat Dill Crisps (p. 78), Melba toast, or sesame crackers.

Makes about 3/4 cup. Recipe may be multiplied.

Marinated Mushrooms

This appetizer will keep in the refrigerator for about a week in a closed jar.

8 ounces medium-sized mushrooms
1/4 cup vegetable oil
1/4 cup olive oil
1/4 cup red wine vinegar
1 clove garlic, peeled
1 tablespoon dried parsley leaves
1 teaspoon dried thyme
1/4 teaspoon salt

Clean the mushrooms and remove the stems. (Reserve stems for another use.) Mix remaining ingredients and pour over the mushrooms. Refrigerate at least overnight before serving.

Serve with toothpicks.

Makes 6 or more servings.

Spiced Pecans

Spiced Pecans may be stored in plastic bags in the freezer for several weeks and thawed just before serving time.

> Raw pecan halves (1/4 cup for each guest)
> Equal parts melted butter and oil
> Salt
> Chili powder or paprika

Preheat the oven to 300°. Spread the pecan halves in a single layer in a shallow pan. Roast, stirring often, until the nuts begin to turn golden, about 20 minutes. Toward the end of the baking, stir in enough butter–oil mixture to coat the nuts very lightly. Sprinkle on salt and chili powder or paprika to taste. Cool.

Homemade Roasted Peanuts

These peanuts may be roasted, cooled, and stored in plastic bags in the freezer. Thaw just before serving time.

> Raw shelled peanuts (1/4 cup for each guest)
> Equal parts melted butter and oil
> Salt

Preheat oven to 300°. Spread peanuts in a single layer in a shallow baking pan. Roast, stirring often, until peanuts turn golden and begin to form little bubbles on the surface. Stir in the butter–oil mixture sparingly in the last few minutes of baking. Peanuts should be barely coated. Sprinkle with salt and cool before serving. Ground sea salt gives a more pleasant, less salty taste.

VEGETABLES,
RICE,
AND
GRITS

Black-eyed Peas with Blue Cheese Dressing

Just to prove black-eyed peas don't have to be cooked with salt pork to be good, try this. It can be made several days ahead of time.

Dried black-eyed peas ($1/2$ cup per person)
1 small onion, chopped
1 cup mayonnaise
$1/3$ cup salad oil
$1/3$ cup catsup
2 tablespoons granulated sugar
2 tablespoons vinegar
1 teaspoon prepared mustard
$1/2$ teaspoon paprika
$1/4$ teaspoon each celery seed and black pepper
Blue cheese to taste

Cook dried black-eyed peas until tender but not until they get so soft they fall apart. The skins should remain intact. The best way to accomplish this is to keep the heat very low throughout the cooking. Drain when cooked.

For dressing, stir together remaining ingredients. Mix with black-eyed peas as needed to make salad. Store remaining dressing in a jar in the refrigerator to use on green salads.

Makes about $2^1/4$ cups dressing.

Three-Bean Salad

Here, convenience and good flavor coincide. I honestly prefer the texture of canned beans for this salad. If you use canned beans, choose unseasoned varieties, and rinse the beans very well. This salad should be prepared at least a day ahead of time.

> 1 small onion, chopped
> 1 clove garlic, peeled
> 1/2 teaspoon salt
> 1/4 cup red wine vinegar
> 2 tablespoons lemon juice
> 2 tablespoons sweet pickle juice
> 2 cups cooked or canned pinto beans
> 1 cup cooked or canned white beans
> 1 cup cooked or canned dark red kidney beans
> 1/3 cup sweet pickle relish
> 1/3 cup chopped pimento
> 1/3 cup chopped parsley

Combine the first six ingredients in a jar. Shake and allow to stand at least an hour.

Combine the beans and cover with dressing. Refrigerate overnight or longer. Just before serving, mix in the pickle relish, pimento, and parsley. Use as a side dish or serve on lettuce leaves as a salad.

Makes about 6 servings.

Sweet Potatoes in Orange Shells

Plan to make this classic favorite after you make Ambrosia (p. 116), when you'll have orange shells left over. The filled shells may be frozen and then thawed and baked later.

8 oranges, halved and scooped out
8 medium sweet potatoes, boiled
1/2 cup butter
3/4 cup brown sugar
4 eggs, beaten
1 cup cream (milk will do)
1–3 teaspoons ground nutmeg
1/4 teaspoon ground cinnamon
1 teaspoon salt
1/2 cup chopped pecans
1/2 cup bourbon whiskey

Preheat oven to 350°.

Half the oranges. Scoop out orange from peeling and set shells aside.

Mash the hot potatoes with the butter. Add brown sugar, eggs, cream, and spices. Stir in the bourbon and pecans. Fill the orange shells with the mixture. Bake for 20 minutes in a 350° oven.

Makes 8 servings.

Eggplant in Tomato Sauce

This dish is especially good for buffets because it should be served at room temperature and it can be made many days ahead of time. It's at its best if you can use eggplant fresh from your garden or the farmer's market, but it turns out well using supermarket eggplant, too, because the tomato sauce counteracts any bitterness that may be in the eggplant.

1 large eggplant
$1/2$ cup + 2 tablespoons olive oil
$2^{1}/2$ cups sliced onion
1 cup sliced celery
2 8-ounce cans tomato sauce
$1/4$ cup red wine vinegar
2 tablespoons granulated sugar
2 tablespoons drained capers (do not omit)
$1/2$ teaspoon salt
12 pitted black olives, sliced

Cut the eggplant into cubes. Do not peel it. Sauté the cubes in $1/2$ cup of the oil until they begin to turn golden. Remove. Add the remaining 2 tablespoons of oil to the pan and sauté the onion and celery until tender but not brown.

Return the eggplant to the skillet. Add tomato sauce. Bring to a boil; lower heat and simmer uncovered for 15 minutes. Add remaining ingredients, cover the pan, and simmer 20 minutes.

Refrigerate at least overnight before serving. Serve at room temperature. Makes 6 generous servings.

Gold Medallion Carrots

Use the freshest, sweetest carrots you can find.

2 bunches carrots, peeled
3 tablespoons butter
2 tablespoons honey
1 tablespoon Dijon mustard
2 tablespoons white wine

Slice carrots in ¼-inch rounds. (A food processor makes short work of this job.) Steam in a small amount of water or cook in microwave until barely tender—about 5 minutes. Drain and reserve any cooking liquid that remains.

In a saucepan or microwave dish heat together the butter, honey, mustard, cooking liquid and wine. Stir until mixed. Add the carrots. *The carrots may be cooked ahead to this point.*

At serving time, heat the carrots in the honey sauce either in the microwave or on stovetop. Cook rapidly to reduce the liquids to a glaze, stirring several times to coat the carrots.

Serve surrounded with Sautéed Spinach (below).

Makes 6 servings.

Sautéed Spinach

The beauty of this recipe, apart from its ease, is that the spinach looks beautifully shiny and green and doesn't develop the oxalic taste that sets your teeth on edge.

2 pounds fresh spinach
3 tablespoons olive oil
Lemon juice
Coarsely ground black pepper

Wash and stem the spinach. Chop coarsely. Refrigerate wrapped in a tea towel until cooking time.

To cook, heat the oil in a heavy skillet or wok. Stir in the spinach. Cook and stir over high heat just until the spinach is limp and tender. Do not overcook.

To prepare in microwave, place spinach in large glass dish with oil. Stir to coat. Add 2 tablespoons water. Cover. Cook on high 6–7 minutes.

Season with lemon juice and coarsely ground black pepper. Serve with Gold Medallion Carrots (above).

Makes 6 servings.

Endive Salad with Bacon Dressing

Originally, of course, bacon dressing was made entirely with bacon fat. You can retain the familiar old flavor but lower the cholesterol by frying the bacon, pouring out the fat and substituting oil.

6 cups endive lettuce, loosely packed
6 slices bacon
3 tablespoons oil
1 small onion, chopped
3 tablespoons cider vinegar
3 tablespoons granulated sugar
Ground pepper

Wash the endive and tear into bite-size pieces. Wrap in a tea towel and refrigerate in a plastic bag until ready to prepare dressing.

To make the dressing, fry the bacon in a heavy skillet until very crisp. Drain the bacon on paper towels and set aside. Pour away the fat that has accumulated in the skillet but do not wash the pan. Add the oil to the pan and over medium heat sauté the onion until it begins to soften slightly. Stir in the vinegar and sugar. Cook and stir until the sugar dissolves. Remove from heat and set aside until serving time.

To serve, pile the endive in a large wooden or pottery bowl. Bring the oil mixture to a boil and immediately pour it over the endive. Toss to coat each piece with dressing and to slightly wilt the endive. Crumple the reserved bacon over the top. Season to taste with ground pepper.

Makes 6 servings.

Cucumber and Onion Marinade

Prepare this marinade several hours before serving time.

3 medium cucumbers
2 sweet Vidalia or Bermuda onions
1/2 cup malt vinegar
Coarse salt
Freshly ground pepper

Peel the cucumbers and onions and slice them thinly. Place in a small bowl with the vinegar and mix. Refrigerate several hours.

At serving time sprinkle lightly with the salt and pepper.

Makes 6 servings.

Rice-Stuffed Vegetables

Rice-Stuffed Vegetables are good served hot or at room temperature. You may prepare them earlier in the day to serve at room temperature, or prepare a day or more earlier to refrigerate and reheat in the microwave.

Allow one or two whole vegetables per person.

Use any or all of the vegetables below for stuffing, depending on what is available. Don't use instant rice for this recipe.

> Green bell peppers
> Fresh tomatoes
> Small eggplant
> Medium yellow or zucchini squash
> Raw white rice (3 tablespoons per whole vegetable)
> Chopped onion (about 1/2 small onion for each vegetable)
> Olive oil
> Salt and pepper
> 1/4 teaspoon granulated sugar for each vegetable
> Freshly chopped parsley
> Basil or thyme
> Red potatoes or any waxy potato, thickly sliced
> Fresh bread crumbs for topping
> 1 cup chopped fresh or canned tomatoes and juice
> Water

Preheat oven to 375°.

Wash all the vegetables.

Remove the tops and seeds from the peppers, reserving the tops.

Hollow out the tomatoes, reserving the juice and pulp. Halve the eggplant and soak in salted water about 20 minutes. Rinse, drain and dry. Halve the zucchini. Scoop out and reserve most of the flesh from the eggplant and zucchini.

Coarsely chop the reserved flesh of the vegetables. Be sure to include all the juices. Stir in raw rice.

Sauté the onion in a little olive oil until transparent and add to the chopped mixture. Mix in salt, pepper, sugar, and a handful of parsley and basil or thyme to taste. *(continued next page)*

Loosely fill each vegetable about two-thirds full with the rice mixture. Pour into each vegetable about a tablespoon of water and as much olive oil as your conscience and taste buds allow—at least a teaspoonful for each vegetable shell. More will taste better and make you fat quicker.

Arrange the stuffed vegetables in a shallow baking dish, wedging in thick slices of potato to hold them upright (I don't peel the potato unless the skin is rough). Sprinkle the tops of the filled vegetables with bread crumbs.

Pour the chopped tomatoes and juice into the bottom of the pan around the vegetables. You should have about 1/2 inch of tomato and liquid in the bottom of the pan. Make up the difference with water if necessary. Drizzle a little more olive oil into the pan.

Bake *uncovered* about 1 hour, or until the rice is tender and the tops are brown, basting the vegetables with pan juices several times.

Serve hot or at room temperature.

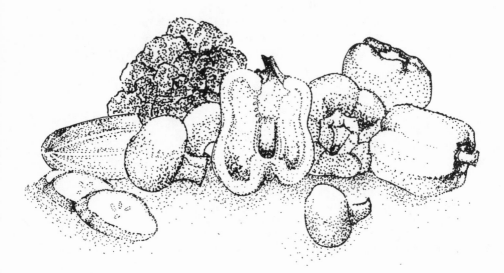

Broccoli Casserole

1 large bunch fresh broccoli or 2 packages frozen broccoli
4 large white onions, peeled and sliced
1 4-ounce jar chopped pimento
$1/4$ cup butter
$1/4$ cup vegetable oil
$1/2$ cup flour
$1^{1}/2$ cups milk
$1^{1}/2$ cups chicken stock
2 tablespoons Dijon mustard
3 tablespoons lemon juice
2 teaspoons granulated sugar
Salt
White pepper
$1/2$ cup grated cheese
$1/2$ cup bread crumbs

Preheat oven to 350°.

Steam or microwave the broccoli until barely tender. Drain. Lightly steam and drain the sliced onions. Drain the pimento. Mix all the vegetables in a baking dish.

Melt the butter and oil in a heavy saucepan. Stir in the flour and continue to stir over medium heat until mixture turns golden. Gradually whisk in the milk and stock, stirring as the sauce cooks and thickens. Season with mustard, lemon juice, sugar, salt and pepper. Pour sauce over the broccoli and onions.

Sprinkle the top with the grated cheese and then with the bread crumbs. *The broccoli may be prepared ahead to this point and refrigerated for several hours.*

To serve, bake for 35–45 minutes, or until casserole is very hot and brown on top. Or cook completely, and reheat, loosely covered, in microwave oven for 10–15 minutes.

Makes 6 servings.

Turnip Casserole

3 cups cooked, mashed turnips, cooled
2 tablespoons butter
3 eggs, beaten
1–2 tablespoons caraway seeds
Salt and pepper
3/4 cup rye bread crumbs

Preheat oven to 350°.

Mix the butter, eggs and caraway seeds into the turnips. Add salt and pepper to taste and stir in. Spoon the mixture lightly into a greased baking dish. Cover the top entirely with bread crumbs and dot with butter. *This casserole may be assembled as much as 24 hours ahead of time and baked when you are ready to serve.*

Bake for 35 minutes or until top is brown and turnips are very hot.

Makes 6 servings.

Wilted Collards

This is a fine alternative to the boil-forever approach.

1/2 pound bacon, diced
1 large onion, chopped
2 garlic cloves, minced
1 tablespoon granulated sugar
2 large bunches collards
Hot pepper vinegar

Sauté the bacon until limp in a large deep pot. Add onion, garlic and sugar. Chop the collards, removing tough stems. Stir the collards into the kettle with the bacon. Cover the pot and steam the collards about 3–4 minutes, or until limp. Uncover, raise heat to high and reduce pan juices. *Collards may be cooked ahead to this point and reheated.* Serve hot with pepper vinegar.

Makes 6 servings.

Rice with Collards

An uncommon use of traditional Southern ingredients, this dish is excellent for buffets.

> 1 cup chopped onion
> 2 cloves garlic, minced
> 2 tablespoons butter
> 2 pounds chopped collards (or frozen)
> 1/4 cup water
> 4 cups cooked rice
> 4 eggs, beaten
> 1 cup milk
> 1 1/2 cups grated cheddar cheese
> 1/4 cup chopped parsley
> Salt to taste
> 1/2 cup chopped raw cashews

Preheat oven to 350°.

Sauté the onions and garlic in the butter until soft. Stir in the collards and cook and stir to coat them with butter. Add the water. Cover the pan and steam until the collards are just tender. You may add more water if necessary, but you probably won't need to, especially if you use frozen collards.

In a large mixing bowl combine the collards with the rice, eggs, milk, cheese, parsley, and salt. Pack into a buttered baking dish and sprinkle with cashews. *The recipe may be prepared several hours ahead to this point.* Bake, covered, for about 35 minutes.

Makes 6 servings.

Green Rice with Cheese

Of all the recipes for green rice that I've tasted, this is my favorite. It has a delicious but pungent garlic flavor that may be inappropriate on some occasions.

> 1 cup raw rice
> 2½ cups water
> ½ teaspoon salt
> 1 large onion, chopped
> 1 green pepper, chopped
> ½ cup chopped fresh parsley
> 1 clove garlic, minced
> ¼ cup salad oil
> 1 cup grated Swiss cheese
> 1 cup milk
> 1 egg, beaten

Preheat oven to 350°.

Put rice in water with salt and cook until tender. (All the water should be absorbed.) Sauté the onion, pepper, parsley and garlic in the oil until soft but not brown. Mix them into the rice. Mix in the grated cheese. Put the rice mixture in a 6-cup baking dish. Combine the milk and egg and pour it over the rice. *The recipe may be prepared several hours ahead to this point.*

Bake, covered, for 1 hour.

Makes 4–6 servings.

Orange Rice Pileau

2 tablespoons butter
2 tablespoons vegetable oil
1 medium onion, chopped
1 cup raw white rice
Grated rind of 1 orange
1¼ cups chicken stock
1 cup fresh or frozen orange juice
Chopped pecans
1 small can mandarin orange segments

Melt the butter and oil in a large saucepan. Sauté the onion until soft and translucent but not brown.

Stir in the rice. Cook and stir over medium heat about 5 minutes, until the rice appears translucent.

Add the orange rind, chicken stock, and orange juice. Bring to a gentle boil. Cover and simmer on low about 25 minutes, until the rice is done and all the liquid has been absorbed.

The rice may be prepared in advance to this point and refrigerated. To reheat, place covered dish in microwave oven for about 5–7 minutes or cover in top of a double boiler over boiling water. Stir with a fork to separate the grains.

To serve, sprinkle chopped pecans on top and garnish with drained mandarin orange segments.

Makes 6 servings.

Carolina Red Rice

¼ pound bacon
1 medium onion, chopped
2 cups rice
1 cup canned tomatoes
1½ cups stock
Tabasco sauce
Salt and pepper

Fry the bacon in a skillet. Remove from the pan and crumble. Sauté the onion in the bacon fat until tender but not brown. Pour off extra fat. Stir in the rice and cook briefly, stirring constantly, until all the rice grains are coated with fat. Add the tomatoes and stock. Season to taste with Tabasco, salt and pepper. Cover and cook over low heat, 35–50 minutes, until the rice is tender. Check after the first 15 minutes and several times thereafter to be sure the rice is not cooking dry. Add stock or water if necessary.

Makes 6–8 generous servings.

Rice Salad

Rice Salad makes a nice change from potato salad. It's a good buffet dish because it holds so well and it can be made a day ahead. It's especially good with cold sliced ham. Even if you normally prefer white rice, use brown in this recipe. It offers better texture for salad.

To serve as a main dish, add 2 cups chopped cooked shrimp and 1 cup frozen baby peas.

> 4 cups cooked long grain brown rice
> 1 large sweet onion, chopped
> 1/4 cup pickle relish
> 4 celery ribs, chopped
> 1 green pepper, chopped
> 1 red pepper, chopped
> 1 cup mayonnaise
> 1 teaspoon golden prepared mustard
> 1/2 teaspoon celery seed
> Salt and pepper to taste
> 1/4 cup sliced green olives
> 4 hard cooked eggs, sliced
> Romaine lettuce, finely shredded

Chill the rice. Mix all the ingredients except the olives, sliced egg, and lettuce. Chill several hours or overnight. Serve surrounded with shredded lettuce, and topped with olives and sliced eggs.

Makes 8 servings.

Golden Cheese Grits

For the most flavorful results, use very fresh, yellow grits, not instant, for this recipe. White grits may be traditional, but yellow grits carry more flavor.

1 cup regular yellow grits
1 cup skim milk
2 cups water
2 tablespoons butter
$1/2$ teaspoon salt
$1/2$ cup grated sharp Cheddar cheese

Combine everything but the cheese in the top part of a double boiler. Place over, not in, boiling water, cover, and cook on medium heat, stirring only occasionally, for about one hour, until grits are soft but not soupy.

Shortly before serving, stir in the cheese and allow the grits to stand until cheese is melted. Once cooked, grits will hold over warm water for up to an hour before serving.

Makes 6 generous servings

Variations

- Spicy Hot Grits: Stir in $1/4$ to $1/2$ cup picante sauce with the cheese.
- Garlic Grits: Omit the cheese. Peel and mash 2 or 3 fresh cloves of garlic and stir them into the cooked grits with 2 additional tablespoons of butter. Allow to stand at least 20 minutes, then remove the garlic cloves.
- Grits Timbales: Use cooked leftover grits, or cook ahead and chill. Shape patties of about $1/2$ cup each, bread them in cornflake crumbs, and brown lightly in a small amount of butter. Good with tomato sauce or gravy.

Garden Relish

Here's an excellent cold vegetable dish to make ahead. Since it will keep in the refrigerator for up to two weeks, you may want to double the recipe.

1/2 head cauliflower, cut into small pieces
2 carrots, peeled and cut into diagonal slices
2 stalks celery, cut into 1-inch pieces
1 green pepper, cut into 2-inch strips
1 red or yellow pepper, cut into 2-inch strips
1 4-ounce jar chopped pimento, drained
1 3-ounce jar pitted green olives, drained
3/4 cup wine vinegar
1/2 cup olive oil
1 tablespoon granulated sugar
1 teaspoon salt
1/4 teaspoon black pepper
1/2 teaspoon dried thyme
1 teaspoon dried dill weed
1/4 cup water

Put all ingredients into a heavy skillet. Bring to a boil; reduce heat. Simmer, covered, for about 5 minutes. Do not overcook. Cool, then refrigerate for at least 24 hours before serving.

Makes about 6 servings.

Cold Vegetable Mélange

10-ounce package frozen green beans
10-ounce package frozen limas
2 cups thin carrot slices
1/4 pound pearl onions, peeled
1 1/2 cups chicken stock
1 bay leaf
1 teaspoon salt
2 tablespoons olive oil
1/4 cup lemon juice
1/4 teaspoon dry mustard
1/4 teaspoon brown sugar
1 small clove garlic
1/4 cup chopped parsley
Salt to taste
Pepper to taste

Combine the vegetables with the stock, bay leaf, and salt in a saucepan. Bring to a simmer and cook, covered, about 10 minutes, or until vegetables are barely tender. (You can do this in the microwave. Start with 10 minutes cooking time and 5 minutes resting time. Add additional time as needed. This won't be any faster than cooking vegetables on the stove top, but it will free the burners for other cooking.) Drain and chill.

Make a dressing by combining the remaining ingredients in a blender or food processor. Pour over the chilled vegetables and marinate at least overnight. *The vegetable mélange may be made up to three days ahead and refrigerated.*

Serve hot or at room temperature.
Makes 6–10 servings.

SOUPS

Cold Fruit Soup

3/4 cups dried apricots
1/2 cup dried pitted prunes
1/2 cup granulated sugar
21/2 cups water
2 tablespoons dark seedless raisins
1/2 lemon, sliced
1 cinnamon stick
1/4 teaspoon whole cloves
1/2 cup Chablis wine
11/2 tablespoons cornstarch
Lemon wedges for garnish

In a large saucepan, combine all the ingredients except the wine, cornstarch, and lemon wedges. Heat to boiling, reduce the heat, and simmer uncovered for 5 minutes, stirring occasionally.

Combine the wine and cornstarch, and gradually stir it into the simmering fruit mixture. Cook, until the soup thickens and the liquid loses its "milky" look. Remove the spices and lemon slices. Refrigerate until very cold. Serve in chilled bowls, garnished with lemon wedges.

This soup can be made a day or two ahead.

Makes 6 small servings.

She-Crab Soup

Don't worry if you can't find crabmeat with roe. Make it He-Crab Soup instead. The soup is *very* rich.

> 1/2 cup butter (do not substitute margarine)
> 2 tablespoons flour
> 4 cups milk
> 2 cups white crabmeat with roe
> 1/2 teaspoons celery salt
> Salt and pepper
> Ground nutmeg
> 1 cup heavy cream, whipped
> 1/4 cup dry sherry

In the top of a metal double boiler melt the butter. Stir in the flour. Cook and stir until mixture is golden. Gradually whisk in milk. Cook until thick and smooth, stirring often.

Add the crabmeat and season to taste with celery salt, pepper, and nutmeg. Cook about 5 minutes longer. *The soup may be made ahead to this point.*

To serve, reheat (if necessary) and stir in the whipped cream, then the sherry. Serve immediately in warm soup bowls.

Makes 6–8 servings.

Peanut Soup

Here's an easy version of a quintessentially Southern soup. Practice saying "quintessentially Southern soup" out loud three times in a row as you're preparing it. The soup is good hot or cold.

> 1 small onion, minced
> 1 rib celery, finely chopped
> 3 tablespoons butter
> 2 teaspoons flour
> 1 quart chicken stock
> 1/2 cup natural (without sugar) chunky peanut butter
> 1 cup cream
> Unsalted roasted peanuts, chopped

In a deep saucepan sauté the onion and celery in the butter until they are soft but not brown. Stir in the flour and cook until the mixture is golden. Gradually stir in the stock. Bring to a boil and simmer until the stock is slightly thickened—about 10 minutes. Stir in the peanut butter, cooking and stirring until it is thoroughly blended in. *The recipe may be prepared ahead to this point if you plan to serve the soup hot.*

At serving time, reheat the soup and stir in the cream. Do not boil once the cream has been added. *To serve cold, stir in the cream and refrigerate. It may be made a day ahead.*

If the soup seems too thick, add a little more stock or cream before you serve it. Garnish with the chopped peanuts.

Makes 6 servings.

Cold Tomato Soup

I've never served this to anyone who hasn't enjoyed it. It couldn't be easier to make, especially if you use a blender.

> 1 cup vegetable cocktail
> 2 cups tomato juice
> ¼ cup tomato purée
> 1 small onion, finely chopped
> 1 teaspoon dried dill weed
> 2 teaspoons grated lemon rind
> 2 tablespoons fresh lemon juice
> ¼ cup chopped parsley
> 2 teaspoons granulated sugar
> 1 cup plain yogurt
> Salt and pepper to taste

Place all ingredients except the yogurt, salt and pepper in the blender jar. Process just enough to mix. Chill. At serving time blend in the yogurt, salt and pepper. Serve in chilled cups nested in a tray of ice.

Makes 6 servings.

Spring Onion Soup

Now that you can buy good green onions in the grocery store almost year-round, you don't necessarily have to wait for spring to serve this good soup. Few soups are easier to prepare.

> 4 cups chicken stock
> 2 cups chopped green onions, including tops and stems
> 1 cup light cream
> Salt and pepper
> Chopped chives or chopped green onions for garnish

Bring the stock to a boil. Add the chopped onions and simmer until they are barely tender, about 5 minutes. Stir in the cream and heat a few minutes longer. Do not boil the soup once you have added the cream. Season to taste with salt and pepper. Serve garnished with chives or chopped onions. *To prepare ahead, do everything but add the cream. Reheat and add cream just before serving.*

Makes 6 servings.

English Pea Soup

In the spring this soup is delicious made with fresh green peas, but it's also very good made with frozen peas. I find it equally good served hot or cold. If you choose to serve the soup cold, you may want to thin it slightly with more stock.

> 3 cups fresh green peas (or 1 1-pound package frozen)
> 2 cups stock
> 2 tablespoons butter
> 1 small onion, minced
> 2 tablespoons flour
> 1 clove garlic, peeled
> 2 teaspoons salt (more or less to taste)
> 1/4 cup dry white wine
> 1 tablespoon granulated sugar (optional)

Simmer the peas in the stock, covered, just until tender. Remove from heat and allow to stand until cool—at least 30 minutes.

Meanwhile, in the soup pan, melt the butter, sauté the onion, then stir in the flour and stir until golden brown. Add the garlic clove.

Drain most of the stock from the peas and pour into the soup pan. With heat on high, cook and stir until the mixture is smooth and bubbling. Add the salt and wine. Cook about 10 minutes longer.

While the stock is cooking, purée the peas in a blender or food processor, reserving about 1/3 cup whole peas for garnish.

Stir the purée into the stock mixture. Taste. If the peas are not very sweet, add the optional sugar now.

The soup may be prepared ahead of time to this point.

When ready to serve, bring just to boiling, pour into a warmed tureen, and garnish with the reserved whole peas.

If you are serving the soup cold, chill the serving bowls and add cold stock to thin the soup (if needed) anytime after the soup has chilled enough for you to judge its thickness.

Makes 5 cups, enough for 6 servings.

Crab and Mushroom Soup

The easiest way to make this oustandingly good soup is in a metal double boiler with a top that can be set directly on the burner. A food processor is helpful for chopping the celery and parsley fine and slicing the mushrooms. Do not put the onion in a food processor because it makes the flavor strong and bitter.

3 tablespoons butter
2 cups finely chopped celery
1/2 cup finely chopped parsley
1 small onion, minced by hand
3 tablespoons flour
1 cup chicken stock
1 cup sliced mushrooms
1 cup crabmeat
1/4 cup sauterne cooking wine
2 cups milk

Melt the butter in the top of the double boiler over direct heat.

Stir in the celery, parsley, and onion. Cook and stir over medium heat until the vegetables are soft and translucent but not brown.

Stir in the flour and cook a few minutes more until the flour begins to be golden.

Whisk in the chicken stock, beating until all lumps are gone from the flour. Set the mixture over hot water in the double boiler and steam for about one hour, until the celery is tender.

Stir in the mushrooms, crabmeat, and wine. *The recipe may be prepared ahead to this point.*

At serving time, add the milk and reheat the soup until it is piping hot. Do not let it cook further once the milk has been added.

Makes 6–8 servings.

FRUITS
AND
FRUIT
DESSERTS

Fresh Fruits

When you serve fresh fruit to guests, it's a little like playing a piano recital. You offer only the perfect pieces.

Though they may not be as evenly colored or uniformly shaped, home-grown fruits usually taste better than commercially produced ones, mainly because they are more likely to be picked when they are ripe. Commercial fruits are often picked green for shipping and then chemically "ripened." Such fruit may look ripe, but it still tastes green.

For those of us who can't grow our own, the local roadside stand is a good alternative. But be sure the stand you patronize really does sell locally grown fruit, picked when ripe; some entrepreneurs buy produce from the same wholesalers who supply supermarkets. Then you pay special prices for what is basically grocery store fruit, and probably went out of your way to do it as well.

Here are a few guidelines for selecting fruit to serve fresh, no matter where you find it.

Apples

Distinguish between cooking and eating-raw apples. The ideal cooking apple is too tart to eat out-of-hand. The crispness we like in an apple for eating raw disintegrates into mush if you cook it.

These apples are good both ways: Granny Smith, MacIntosh, Yellow Transparent, and Rome. Red and Golden Delicious are better raw.

Apples lose moisture and get mealy in home storage, but those stored commercially hold good quality longer.

Apricots, Nectarines, and Peaches

The skins of these should be unbruised, the fruit firm but not hard, the basic undercolor a creamy yellow. Even though the "blush" on these fruits varies in shades of red and rose, the creamy yellow on the rest of the skin is more important. It indicates the presence of sugar—hence sweet fruit. No matter how the color changes, if the yellow isn't present on the skin, the fruit will never be sweet.

Blueberries

Thanks to hybridization and commercial cultivation, blueberries have changed a lot and become more readily available than they once were. My early memories are of huckleberries, which you had to get up early and go into swampy places to pick.

The huckleberries we brought home were smaller than today's com-mercial blueberries, with more intense flavor. But the commercial blueber-ries, being larger, have more edible pulp for the amount of skin you have to contend with. Whether you pick wild huckleberries or buy commercial blueberries, look for fully ripe, plump berries. A deep purple signifies ripe-ness. If the berries are in baskets, look at the bottom of the basket to make sure no juice has leaked through, indicating crushed or rotting berries.

Blueberries will keep for several days in the refrigerator. Do not wash until you are ready to use them.

Cantaloupe

A fully ripe cantaloupe smells like a cantaloupe. A green one doesn't have much smell. The shell should be firm, with uniform netting. Some varieties have a distinct greenish color even when ripe, so don't go by color alone. If it is still slightly green when you buy it, a cantaloupe will ripen on a cupboard shelf.

Grapes

The best way to tell about any grape is to taste it. I suppose you could get yourself kicked out of the farmers' market if you carried this to extremes; but since even a pretty grape can be sour, depending on how and where it was grown, I vote for the taste test.

Pears

Conventional wisdom is that you should pick pears while they are still green and hold them at 70° to ripen at home. Unfortunately, when you buy pears, you have no idea what condition they were in when picked. I've found it better to buy pears that are full-colored in whatever is natural for the variety and already soft enough for eating. Otherwise, they tend to rot from the inside out while you try to ripen them at home.

Pineapple

The standard test for fresh pineapple is to pluck a leaf from the crown. If it comes out easily, the pineapple is ripe. Now, some grocery stores have special pineapple-coring machines so that you can select a pineapple that has been peeled, cored and bagged. I've had excellent luck buying these and probably use three times as much pineapple now that I don't have to struggle with the peeling and coring mess.

Plums

Plums are a joy because, as long as they are firm and unbruised when you buy them, they ripen reliably in the cupboard at home. As soon as they are properly ripe, refrigerate them. They keep longer than most fruits under refrigeration.

Raspberries

Always check the bottom of the container when you buy raspberries. Often they are crushed by their own weight and turn soft and moldy on the bottom, even though they look good on top. Because they're expensive and they don't save well, eat them as soon as you can—or you'll end up with expensive mush.

Strawberries

Again, ripening on the plant is the only way to get a really sweet strawberry. If the berries are light orange or have areas of white when you buy them, they won't ripen or get sweeter—they will simply get mushy and rot. Choose red berries that still have fresh, green, caps intact. Strawberries

don't store well; eat them as soon as you can. Don't wash or hull until ready to use, and store in a cool place—not the refrigerator.

Sweet Cherries

Choose cherries of full color, usually deep purple or maroon, free of hard spots or soft holes in the skin. Refrigerate cherries as soon as you buy them.

Watermelon

The time-honored way to choose a watermelon was once to cut out a plug and taste it. If it tasted good, you used the melon. It's still the best way, but if you cut out a plug today, I think the merchant would cut off your hand. The sweetest melons are those that have ripened on the vine. A sign of this is a recessed and hardened scar where the melon grew from the vine. It's easier to find a ripe melon that has been locally grown than it is some other fruits. Farmers often sell them by the truckload alongside the road, frequently right next to the field in which they grew them. And supermarkets will use local watermelons even when they import other fruits.

Ambrosia

You can't have a Southern cookbook without ambrosia. The most authentic version is simple—just peeled orange segments, grated coconut, and a speck of powdered sugar, layered in a bowl and chilled.

Sometimes it's fun to try a more elaborate combination. Here are two variations.

Ambrosia II

2 cups peeled orange segments, cut in pieces
2 cups crushed pineapple, canned in its own juice
1/2 cup shredded coconut (preferably fresh or frozen)
1/4 cup pineapple juice from the can
1/4 cup orange juice
2 tablespoons honey
1 teaspoon whole cloves

Put the orange segments into a large bowl. Drain the pineapple, reserving the juice, and add it to the oranges. Stir in the coconut, pineapple juice, orange juice and honey. Stir in the cloves. Refrigerate for an hour or more before serving.

Makes 6 servings.

Ambrosia III

2 cups peeled orange segments, cut in pieces
1 cup crushed pineapple, canned in its own juice
1/2 cup shredded coconut (preferably fresh or frozen)
1/2 cup pecan chunks
1 banana, sliced
1 cup miniature marshmallows
1/4 cup orange juice
2 tablespoons honey
1/4 cup sour cream
Fresh mint for garnish

Put the orange segments in a large bowl. Drain the pineapple, reserving 1/4 cup of the juice. Add the pineapple to the oranges. Stir in the coconut, pecans, banana and marshmallows.

Beat together the reserved pineapple juice, orange juice, honey and sour cream. Pour over the fruits. Refrigerate for an hour or more before serving. Garnish with mint leaves.

Makes 6–8 servings.

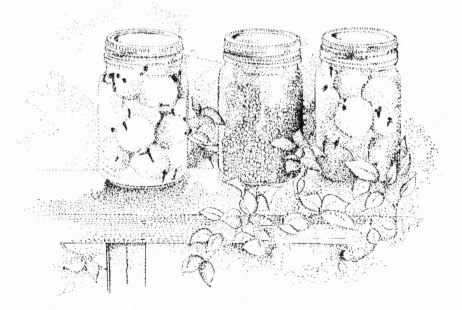

Glazed Sliced Oranges

This dish is nice for dessert after a big meal or with brunch. It can be prepared two or three days ahead of time and refrigerated.

6 oranges
3 cups granulated sugar
1³/₄ cups water
Zest of 2 oranges
¹/₂ cup cranberry juice cocktail

With a potato peeler or zester, strip off the thin outer layer, or zest, of the orange peel.

With a knife, remove the peel and white outer membrane from the oranges. Cut each orange into 4 slices. Set aside.

In a saucepan, combine the sugar, water, orange zest and cranberry juice cocktail. Bring the mixture to a boil. Cook and stir until the sugar is dissolved. Remove from heat and cool. Pour over the orange slices and refrigerate at least overnight before serving.

Serve in clear glass dishes or tall-stemmed glasses.

Makes 6 servings.

Baked Bananas with Strawberry Flambé

This creation makes its own sauce as it bakes. If you are in a hurry or want to keep things simple, omit the flambé step.

6 medium-sized bananas
1 tablespoon soft butter
30 whole strawberries, fresh or frozen
¼ cup brown sugar
¼ cup Grand Marnier (optional)

Preheat oven to 350°.

Peel the bananas and arrange them, whole, side by side in a buttered baking dish. Lightly spread the butter on top of the bananas. Rinse and hull the strawberries if they are fresh. Arrange them in rows in the spaces between the bananas. Sprinkle the brown sugar over the berries and bananas.

Bake for about 25 minutes, or until the bananas are just cooked through. Do not overbake.

To serve flambéed, warm the Grand Marnier and pour it over the bananas and berries. Light immediately. For the most impressive effect, do this at the table with the lights dim so the flame will show. Serve as soon as the fire goes out.

Makes 6 servings.

Brandied Peaches

2 large (29-ounce) cans peach halves
1 cup granulated sugar
½ cup cognac
1 cup liquid from peaches

Drain the peaches, reserving a cup of the liquid, and set them aside. In a saucepan, combine the sugar, cognac and reserved liquid. Bring to a boil and simmer just until the sugar dissolves. Remove from heat and add the peaches. Cool.

Store in a covered container in the refrigerator at least 24 hours before serving. The peaches will keep for many weeks. If the brandy flavor seems to have dimmed, add a few spoonfuls at serving time.

Serve brandied peaches cold as an accompaniment to roast meats and fowl, as a dessert sauce with cake or ice cream, and as a topping for oven pancakes.

Honeydew Melon with Cranberry Jelly

The bright red gleam of the cranberry gelatin contrasts with the soft green of the melon balls, and the tartness of the cranberry balances the sweetness of the honeydew. A beautiful dessert!

> 2 cups bottled cranberry juice cocktail
> 1 envelope unflavored gelatin
> 2 cups fresh honeydew melon balls

Heat the cranberry cocktail just to boiling. Remove from the heat and dissolve the gelatin in it. Pour into an 8-inch square pan and refrigerate until the gelatin is firm.

At serving time, put the melon balls into a clear glass serving dish, reserving a few for garnish. Cut the gelatin into little squares, and mound on top of the melon. Arrange the reserved melon balls on top of the gelatin as a garnish.

To prepare ahead of time, have the melon balls and gelatin squares ready in separate dishes. Combine in the serving dish just before you serve.

Variations

- Honeydew Halves Filled with Cranberry Jelly: Double the gelatin recipe and allow it to cool after mixing. Instead of scooping out the flesh of the honeydew, scoop out only the seeds of a *large* honeydew and pour the cooled gelatin into the centers of the melon halves. Chill until firm. To serve, bring the melon halves to the table and scoop some melon and gelatin into individual serving dishes at the table.
- Watermelon with Wine Jelly: Substitute sauterne for the cranberry juice and watermelon balls for the honeydew.

Fresh Fruit Skewers

Here's a convenient way to make fresh fruit special for the buffet. The skewer combinations here are my favorites, but they should serve only as suggestions, not limitations. If you use fruits such as peaches and apples, which tend to darken after being cut, sprinkle them with lemon juice.

Use the small bamboo skewers that are sold in Oriental food stores and gourmet sections of grocery stores. Allow about 2–3 skewers per person. Serve dipping sauces in tiny containers such as Chinese tea cups.

Skewer Combinations

- White grapes–Strawberries–Pineapple cubes
- Apple wedges–Orange segments–Sweet cherries
- Apricot halves–Red grapes–Persimmon quarters
- Watermelon–Cantaloupe–Honeydew

Dipping Sauces

- Equal amounts of warmed honey and lemon juice
- White crème de menthe sprinkled with grated coconut
- Equal amounts of chocolate liqueur and cream
- Two parts kirsch and 1 part Cointreau
- Two tablespoons butter melted with 2 tablespoons brown sugar
- Maple syrup mixed with a few spoonfuls of strong coffee

Iced Cherries

This service promotes cherries as a special treat. Fill good-sized dessert dishes half full with cracked ice just before serving time. Allowing about ten cherries for each serving, arrange the cherries in the ice with the stems sticking up so that diners can pick them up with their fingers. Serve with small bowls of powdered sugar for dipping.

Iced Raspberries

On those rare occasions when you can pick or buy enough raspberries to share, treat them like jewels. Allow about 1/2 cup raspberries for each serving. Fill the bottom half of shrimp cocktail glasses with cracked ice. Settle the serving cups into the ice, and fill with raspberries. Serve garnished with a slice of lime.

Gilded Fruit

When you can find perfect grapes and berries, make this.

> 1 egg white
> Grapes and berries
> Granulated sugar

Whip the egg white with a fork until it is frothy. Dip each grape and berry into the egg white, roll it in the sugar, and then set it on a cookie sheet to dry.

To serve, cluster the grapes and berries in small bowls to be eaten with fingers, or use the gilded fruits to garnish ice cream. Arranged on large platters, these grapes and berries are good on the buffet.

Minted Fresh Apricots

1/3 cup granulated sugar
1/3 cup fresh lime juice
2 tablespoons chopped fresh mint
3 cups sliced fresh apricots
Mint for garnish

Combine the sugar, lime juice, and 2 tablespoons mint in a saucepan. Bring to a boil. Strain and cool. Pour the mixture over the apricots. Chill for 2–3 hours or overnight. Serve in sherbet glasses garnished with fresh mint.
Makes 6 servings.

Pineapple Baked Apples

6 large baking apples
2 tablespoons lemon juice
1 cup unsweetened pineapple juice
1/3 cup butter
3/4 cup granulated sugar
1 teaspoon ground cinnamon
2 whole cloves

Preheat oven to 350°.
Wash, core, and quarter the apples. Do not peel. Spread the apples in a shallow baking dish. Sprinkle with the lemon juice.
Make a syrup by boiling together the pineapple juice, butter, sugar, cinnamon and cloves.
Pour enough of the syrup over the apples so that they are *almost* covered, reserving any leftover syrup. Stir to coat all the apples with the syrup.
Bake about 30 minutes, until the apples are soft and glazed. Add more syrup (or a little water if you run out of syrup) during baking if necessary to keep the apples slightly moist. *The apples may be prepared a day ahead and refrigerated.* Serve hot or at room temperature.
Makes 6 servings.

Cranberry–Apple Sauce

You can make this anytime the cranberries and apples are available. It freezes perfectly and also keeps well covered in the refrigerator for up to two weeks. When you see cranberries in the grocery store, it's a good idea to freeze a bag or two for later.

> 12 medium apples, preferably tart
> 1 cup fresh or frozen cranberries
> 1/2 cup apple juice or cider
> Honey
> Fresh lemon juice
> Ground cinnamon

Quarter the apples. Wash the cranberries. Place both in a large saucepan with the cider. Cover the pot and simmer for about 30 minutes, stirring occasionally to keep the apples from sticking. When the apples are soft and the cranberries have burst open, force them through a sieve or food mill to separate the skins from the fruit. Sweeten to taste with honey. Season with lemon juice. Sprinkle with cinnamon.

Makes about 6 cups.

BREADS

Biscuits

Biscuits are the subject of more mystique than just about any other Southern food I can think of. I've tasted every kind imaginable—big, small, fat, thin, soft, crusty—and can only conclude that it's very hard to find a *bad* biscuit in the South.

Unlike most other breads, biscuits don't freeze or reheat well. You can easily mix them up ahead except for combining the liquid and dry ingredients to reduce the last-minute work, but biscuits definitely should be served fresh from the oven.

As for convincing guests that your biscuits are divine, just act as though they are and I guarantee, people will believe.

Crisp Biscuits

2 cups flour
3 teaspoons baking powder
1/2 teaspoon salt
6 tablespoons shortening
3/4 cup milk

Preheat oven to 450°.

Sift together the flour, baking powder and salt into a large bowl. Cut in the shortening until the mixture resembles coarse meal. Stir in the milk. Turn the dough out into a floured bowl, knead lightly for a few seconds to form a ball, then quickly pat out to a thickness of about 1/2 inch. Cut with a small biscuit cutter or a 6-ounce juice-concentrate can. Place the biscuits several inches apart on a greased cookie sheet. Bake for about 10 minutes, until the biscuits are light brown. Serve hot.

To prepare ahead, do everything but add the milk. Refrigerate. When ready to bake, stir in the milk and finish the shaping and baking process.

Makes about 12 biscuits.

Angel Biscuits

If a television commercial for a certain paper product weren't already using the line, I'd say these biscuits were made by clouds. They're out of the ordinary because they're so fluffy—not surprising considering they include *three* separate leavening ingredients. Dough for Angel Biscuits can be kept in the refrigerator for a week or more.

> 5 cups all-purpose flour
> 3 tablespoons granulated sugar
> 3 teaspoons baking powder
> 1 teaspoon baking soda
> 1 teaspoon salt
> 3/4 cup shortening
> 1 envelope (1 tablespoon) active dry yeast
> 1/2 cup warm water
> 2 cups buttermilk

Sift together the flour, sugar, baking powder, baking soda and salt.

Cut in the shortening until the mixture resembles coarse meal.

Dissolve the yeast in warm water and stir it into the buttermilk.

Pour the buttermilk–yeast mixture into the dry ingredients and stir until moistened.

Cover and chill.

To bake, preheat oven to 400°. Roll the dough on a floured surface to 1/2-inch thickness. Cut biscuits with a large (2–3 inches) biscuit cutter or a fluted cookie cutter and arrange on a lightly greased cookie sheet. Bake about 12 minutes.

Makes about 4 1/2 dozen biscuits.

Georgia Riz Biscuits

Here's another version of triple-leavened biscuits. This recipe makes fewer than the preceding one.

2½ cups flour
1 teaspoon baking powder
½ teaspoon salt
½ teaspoon baking soda
1 tablespoon granulated sugar
¼ cup shortening
½ envelope active dry yeast
1 cup buttermilk, at room temperature
3 tablespoons melted butter

Sift first five ingredients together into a large bowl. Cut in the shortening until mixture resembles coarse meal. Dissolve the yeast in the buttermilk. Stir the buttermilk into the dry indredients, mixing well.

Turn the dough out onto a floured board, knead a few seconds, and pat out very thin, about ¼ inch. Brush the top of the biscuit dough with melted butter and cut with a biscuit cutter. Arrange half the biscuits on a greased baking sheet so they are not touching each other. Place the remaining pieces on top of those on the sheet. Allow to rise in a warm place for about 1 hour. *To prepare ahead, complete the recipe but hold the shaped biscuits in the refrigerator for as much as 2 hours before moving them into a warm place to rise.*

To bake, preheat oven to 400°. Bake about 10–12 minutes, or until the biscuits are golden brown.

Makes about 12 biscuits.

Soda Biscuits

Some folks with discerning tastes don't like the flavor of modern-day double-acting baking powder. If you're among them, try this old-time recipe.

> 2 cups flour
> 1/2 teaspoon baking soda
> 1 1/2 teaspoons cream of tartar
> 1/4 teaspoon salt
> 2 tablespoons shortening
> 1 cup milk

Preheat oven to 400°.

Sift the dry ingredients together into a large bowl. Cut in the shortening until the mixture resembles coarse meal. Stir in the milk. Turn the dough out onto a floured board and lightly work it into a ball. Pat it out to a thickness of 1 inch. Cut the biscuits with a biscuit cutter or a 6-ounce orange juice concentrate can. Arrange them on a greased cookie sheet so they are not touching. *To prepare ahead, do everything but mixing together the liquid and dry ingredients. Mix, shape, and bake just before serving.* Bake about 10 minutes or until lightly browned.

Makes about 12 biscuits.

Sourdough Biscuits

You need sourdough starter to make these biscuits, but you can easily make up a starter with dried yeast if you don't already have one lurking in a corner of the refrigerator. The biscuits are unbelievably easy to make and, in my family, preferred among all biscuits. It's nice to know they don't contain any shortening. They're crunchy on the outside and light on the inside.

> 2 cups Homemade Sourdough Starter (below)
> 2 cups all-purpose unbleached white flour
> 1 tablespoon granulated sugar
> 1 tablespoon baking powder
> 1/2 teaspoon salt

In a large mixing bowl, bring the starter to room temperature. It can stand for several hours if you get busy with something else.

About an hour before you want to serve the biscuits, sift together the dry ingredients into the bowl with the starter. Mix to make a firm dough.

Working with well-buttered hands, pinch off pieces of dough and shape into balls about the size of golf balls.

Arrange them side by side in a well-greased 12-inch iron skillet, and preheat oven to 400°.

Place biscuits in a warm place for about 20 minutes, or until the biscuits begin to rise. This happens faster than with most yeast mixtures because of the baking powder reacting with the sourdough starter.

Bake for about 30 minutes, or until well browned and crusty. Serve hot. Makes about 24 biscuits.

Homemade Sourdough Starter

> 1 envelope active dry yeast
> 2 cups unbleached white flour
> 1 1/2 cups warm water
> 1 tablespoon honey

Mix the ingredients in a plastic or crockery container large enough to allow the mixture to triple. Cover loosely and allow to stand for about a day, until the mixture is frothy and full of bubbles.

After the mixture has fermented, stir down and refrigerate covered but not sealed tight.

When you use starter, replace what you've taken out with equal amounts of flour and water.

Sweet Potato Biscuits

Funny thing about sweet potato biscuits. Practically everyone remembers them as something grandmother baked; hardly anyone can find a recipe. We conducted a little search for the perfect sweet potato biscuit and came up with several recipes that pleased us. Sometimes sweet potato biscuits brown on the outside before they're done on the inside, probably because of the unpredictable moistness of the sweet potato. Try a batch or two before you make these for a party. When you do prepare them for a party, get everything ready ahead of time, keeping liquid and dry ingredients separate so that all you have to do at the last minute is mix, shape, and bake.

Rosetta Phillips' Sweet Potato Biscuit

2 cups soft white flour
2 teaspoons baking powder
$1/2$ teaspoon salt
Ground nutmeg to taste
$1/2$ cup vegetable shortening
$1/2$ cup milk
1 cup mashed cooked sweet potato

Preheat oven to 400°.

Sift the flour, baking powder, salt, and nutmeg together in a large bowl. Cut in the shortening until the mixture resembles coarse meal.

Stir together the milk and sweet potato, then mix into the flour. Add additional flour as needed to make a dough you can handle. It will not be as stiff as regular biscuit dough. Do not overmix.

Shape the biscuits by hand (rather than cutting them) and arrange on a lightly greased cookie sheet. Bake for about 10 minutes, or until golden brown.

Makes 8–10 small biscuits.

Mrs. Wheeler's Sweet Potato Biscuits

2 cups hot mashed sweet potatoes
1/2 cup butter
1/2 cup granulated sugar
1 teaspoon salt
3 cups flour
3 teaspoons baking powder

Preheat oven to 425°.

Stir the butter and sugar into the hot potatoes. Sift in the dry ingredients and mix well. Roll or flatten the dough with your hands and cut into biscuits. Arrange, not touching, on a lightly greased baking sheet. Bake about 8–10 minutes, or until golden brown.

Makes about 20 biscuits, depending on size.

Mrs. Carroll's Sweet Potato Biscuits

This recipe comes from Marion Brown's classic *Southern Cook Book.*

2 cups boiled, mashed sweet potatoes
1 tablespoon butter
2 cups flour
1 tablespoon granulated sugar
1 teaspoon salt
1/4 teaspoon baking soda
Buttermilk

Preheat oven to 400°.

Stir the butter into the warm sweet potatoes. Sift in the dry ingredients. Add buttermilk as needed to make a dough you can handle. Roll out the dough or flatten with your hands. Cut with a biscuit cutter. Arrange on a lightly greased baking sheet and bake 10–15 minutes, or until done through and golden brown.

Makes about 20 biscuits, depending on size.

Carol LeCompte's Sweet Potato Biscuits

This is probably my favorite of the sweet potato biscuit recipes. Walter Lambert included it in his collection of recollections and recipes, *Kinfolks and Custard Pie*, saying that although they weren't part of his personal culinary tradition in East Tennessee, they were so good he put them in his book anyway. It differs from the previous recipes in that it uses a baked, rather than boiled, sweet potato.

> 1 small sweet potato, baked and peeled
> 2 tablespoons butter
> 1 cup flour
> 2 teaspoons baking powder
> $1/4$ teaspoon salt
> 3–4 tablespoons milk

Preheat oven to 400°.

Mash the sweet potato with the butter and cool. Sift the dry ingredients into the potato, then stir in enough milk to make a dough you can handle. Put the dough onto a floured board, shape it into a ball, and pat or roll it out. Cut biscuits with a biscuit cutter. Arrange on a greased baking pan and bake 10–12 minutes, or until brown.

Makes 12 biscuits.

Homemade Biscuit Mix

It's nice to have this mix around when you want to mix up biscuits in a hurry. Unlike commercial mixes, it contains no preservatives with strange-sounding names, and I think it tastes better.

> 3 cups self-rising flour
> 1 $1/2$ teaspoons baking powder
> 1 tablespoon granulated sugar
> 1 cup shortening

Sift the dry ingredients together into a large bowl. Cut in the shortening until the mixture resembles coarse meal. Keep covered in the refrigerator for up to 4 weeks.

To bake, preheat oven to 450°. Stir in enough milk to make a soft dough and proceed as with other recipes. Bake 8–10 minutes.

Each cup of mix makes about 6 2-inch biscuits.

Muffins

White Cornmeal Muffins

I like to serve these muffins with a substantial meal of poultry or pork. They're crunchy on the outside but moist and tender inside. Even if you don't generally make cornbread with sugar, don't omit the tablespoon of sugar in this recipe. It makes the muffins taste as though they're baked with fine cornmeal fresh from the mill. Guests tend to eat them, one after another, until they're gone, but the leftovers, if you should ever be able to manage any, make good cornbread stuffing.

> 2¼ cups fine white cornmeal
> 3 teaspoons baking powder
> 2 teaspoons salt
> 1 teaspoon baking soda
> 1 tablespoon granulated sugar
> 2 eggs
> 2 cups buttermilk
> ¼ cup melted butter

Preheat oven to 450°.

In a large mixing bowl, stir together the cornmeal, baking power, salt, baking soda and sugar.

Beat the eggs and combine with the buttermilk and melted butter. *The muffins may be prepared ahead up to this point, so long as liquid ingredients are refrigerated.*

Pour liquids into dry ingredients and stir with a spoon until thoroughly mixed. Spoon batter into buttered muffin tins.

Bake about 10 minutes.

Makes about 12 medium muffins.

Yellow Cornmeal Muffins

Try these substantial, sweet muffins for breakfast or tea when you want the bread to be a main part of the meal. They're tender and springy inside, quite different from the traditional dense cornbread most of us are accustomed to.

1 cup yellow cornmeal
1 cup unbleached white flour
2 teaspoons baking powder
1/2 teaspoon baking soda
1/2 teaspoon salt
1/4 cup honey
11/4 cup buttermilk
1 egg, beaten
1/4 cup butter, melted

Preheat oven to 425°.

Sift together the cornmeal, flour, baking powder, baking soda and salt into a large bowl.

Combine the honey, buttermilk, egg and butter. *The muffins may be prepared ahead up to this point, so long as liquid ingredients are refrigerated.*

Pour liquids into dry ingredients and mix gently but thoroughly. Do not overmix or the corn muffins will be tough.

Spoon the batter into buttered muffin cups. Bake about 10 minutes.

Makes about 12 medium muffins.

Hemlock Inn's Bran Muffins

So many guests at the Hemlock Inn in Bryson City, North Carolina, ask for this recipe that the proprietors, John and Ella Jo Shell, have had it printed on recipe cards to distribute to all who hope to duplicate the muffins at home. They're a glory for entertaining because the batter will keep for two months in the refrigerator. Also, bran muffins freeze perfectly and are excellent reheated in the microwave.

> 3 cups white granulated sugar
> 5 cups flour
> 1 15-ounce package raisin bran
> 5 teaspoons baking soda
> 1 teaspoon salt
> 4 eggs, lightly beaten
> 1 quart buttermilk
> 2 cups melted butter or margarine

Mix the dry ingredients in a *very* large bowl. Mix the wet ingredients together and stir them into the dry ones. Keep in a covered bowl (or commercial-sized mayonnaise jar) in the refrigerator.

To bake, preheat oven to 400°. Fill greased muffin cups about two-thirds full. Add pecans or more raisins if you wish. Bake about 20 minutes. Serve hot, of course.

Makes about 3 quarts of batter.

Old-Time Bran Muffins

The batter for these muffins can be kept in the refrigerator for up to six weeks. This recipe differs from the previous one in that it calls for old-fashioned miller's bran, the natural, unprocessed bran just as it comes off the wheat berry. If your grocer doesn't have it, tell him it can be ordered from Hodgson Mill. Many natural-food stores carry it also.

>1 cup unprocessed bran
>1 cup boiling water
>1 cup brown sugar
>1/2 cup butter or margarine
>2 eggs, lightly beaten
>2 cups unprocessed bran
>2 1/2 cups unbleached white flour
>1/2 teaspoon baking soda
>1 teaspoon salt
>2 cups buttermilk

Preheat oven to 400°.

In a large bowl, pour the boiling water over 1 cup of bran. Stir and allow to stand. In another bowl, cream together the sugar, butter and eggs. Stir this mixture into the bran in the large bowl. Add the remaining 2 cups of bran. Sift in the flour, baking soda and salt. Stir in the buttermilk. Mix well. Store in a tightly covered container in the refrigerator. If the batter darkens, stir it before using.

To bake, stir the batter well and fill greased muffin tins about two-thirds full. Add raisins or blueberries if you like. Bake about 20 minutes. Serve hot.

Makes about 2 1/2 quarts batter.

> *Variations*
> - Blueberry–Bran Muffins: Add unsweetened frozen blueberries to batter.
> - Raisin–Bran Muffins: Add raisins to batter.

Yeast Breads

Whole Wheat Bread

No kneading! Of all the yeast breads I bake, this is the easiest, most versatile and most flavorful. Sliced very thin, it's especially good with spreads as an appetizer. It freezes beautifully and will keep up to a week tightly wrapped in the refrigerator without getting dry.

To get the best texture with this recipe, let the batter stand as much as 15 or 20 minutes several times during the mixing process. This develops the gluten and makes a more springy finished bread. Use flour with finely ground bran.

> 1 envelope active dry yeast
> 1 tablespoon granulated sugar
> 1/4 cup warm water
> 2 cups warm water
> 1 teaspoon salt
> 3 tablespoons oil
> 6 tablespoons honey
> 5 cups whole wheat flour
> 1/2 cup nonfat dried milk powder

In a large mixing bowl, dissolve the yeast and the sugar in the 1/4 cup warm water. Allow to stand until the mixture begins to bubble.

Add the 2 cups warm water, salt, oil and honey.

Beat in about half the flour, a cup at a time. (After this is a good time to let the dough stand for a while as you do something else.)

Beat in the milk powder, a little at a time. (Now you can let the dough stand again.)

Beat in the rest of the flour and continue beating until the dough is shiny and elastic. The more you've let the mixture stand in between mixing steps the easier this last step will be.

When the mixture is shiny you can let it stand again or immediately divide it into greased pans. Use two pans—5 × 9" or slightly smaller—or several individual-loaf pans. For nicely shaped loaves the dough should fill the pans by about half.

Allow to rise in a warm place until nearly doubled in bulk. Do not over-rise or the texture will be coarse.

Bake in a preheated 400° oven for 35–45 minutes.

Remove loaves from pans and cool on racks as soon as the bread comes out of the oven. This bread tastes better cool than hot.

Makes 2 regular loaves or 4 individual loaves.

Refrigerator Potato Bread

Refrigerator Potato Bread dough will keep, ready to use, in the refrigerator for up to ten days. It's a great convenience and a versatile, tasty bread for sandwich loaves, dinner rolls or breakfast sweet rolls.

> 1 large potato
> 1 teaspoon salt
> 1 cup water
> 1/2 cup butter
> 1/2 cup granulated sugar
> 1/2 cup dry milk
> 3 eggs
> 2 envelopes active dry yeast
> 1/2 cup warm water
> 2 teaspoons granulated sugar
> 5–6 cups unbleached white or bread flour

Peel the potato, cut it up and boil in salted water until tender. Mash the potato while it is still hot, making sure to get rid of all lumps. Mix in the butter and 1/2 cup sugar. As the mixture cools, add the milk powder and eggs. Stir thoroughly.

Dissolve the yeast in the 1/2 cup warm water with the 2 teaspoons sugar. When it starts to bubble, put it into a large bowl with the potato mixture. Begin stirring in flour, beating hard with a wooden spoon, until you have a dough you can handle.

Turn the dough out onto a floured board, form into a ball and let it stand for about 15 minutes. Knead, adding more flour if necessary, until smooth and elastic.

Place the kneaded dough into a large greased bowl, cover with a damp cloth, and allow to rise until doubled in bulk.

To store, knead the dough down, cover the bowl with plastic wrap, and refrigerate. The dough has a tendency to creep out of the bowl, so either weight it down with a plate or knead it back down every day or so.

To use, let the dough rise at room temperature until about doubled in bulk again, usually about 2 hours. Knead it down again and shape into loaves or rolls. Let rise until doubled in bulk.

Baking times depend on the size of the breads. Bake rolls at 400° for 20–30 minutes, or until lightly browned and cooked through; bake loaves at 350° about 1 hour.

Makes 2 average-sized loaves or about 4 dozen rolls.

Variation

- Herbed Potato Rolls: Knead in 1 table-spoon dried parsley and 1 teaspoon dried thyme as you shape rolls.

Crusty Wheat Bread

This is the most patient bread dough in the world. You can mix it up from beginning to end without stopping, or if you have other things to do, you can let it stand between steps without hurting anything. If anything, the flavor improves.

> 4 envelopes active dry yeast
> 5 cups lukewarm water
> 2 tablespoons oil
> 1 tablespoon honey
> 1 tablespoon salt
> 5 cups unbleached white or bread flour
> 5 cups whole wheat flour
> 3–5 cups additional white flour

In a large bowl, combine the yeast, water, oil, honey and salt. Beat in the 5 cups white flour. Allow the mixture to bubble from 1 to 10 hours.

When you are ready to continue, mix in the whole wheat flour. Knead in more white flour, until you have a dough you can handle. Allow it to stand 15 minutes to 1 hour.

To continue, knead until smooth and elastic. Allow to rise until double in bulk. *Punch down and allow to rise again if it is not convenient to bake the bread yet, or skip this and shape the loaves.*

Shape into 5 long, rope-like loaves. Arrange them on a greased cookie sheet. Make three diagonal slashes in the top of each loaf. Brush with water.

Put the loaves into a cold oven. Turn the oven to warm and watch the bread closely. As soon as it starts to rise, raise the heat to 400° and bake until the crust is brown, about 25 minutes, spraying or brushing water on the bread once or twice during baking. *These loaves may be frozen and thawed to reheat at serving time.*

Makes 5 long loaves.

DESSERTS

Mother's Angel Food Cake

Once you've tasted a homemade angel food cake, I promise you'll never settle for the cake-mix version again. The difference is stunning.

Mother says brown eggs make a higher cake than white ones, and, of course, the fresher they are the better. For the highest cake possible, have the egg whites at room temperature and don't let even a speck of yolk get into the whites.

I can remember when Mother made angel food cake with a hand egg beater, but she uses an electric mixer now.

> 12 egg whites
> 1 1/2 teaspoons cream of tartar
> 3/4 cup granulated sugar
> 1 1/2 teaspoons vanilla extract
> 1 cup sifted cake flour
> 1 1/4 cups sifted powdered sugar

Preheat oven to 375°.

Mix the egg whites and cream of tartar in a large bowl. Beat at high speed until the egg whites are foamy. Continue beating, adding the granulated sugar a spoonful at a time. Beat continuously until the sugar is dissolved and you can not feel any graininess when you rub a dab of the meringue between your thumb and finger. The whites should be glossy and stand in soft peaks. Beat in the vanilla extract.

Sift the already sifted cake flour and powdered sugar together twice. Sift this mixture over the egg whites, about 1/2 cup at a time. Gently fold in the dry ingredients with a spatula after each sifting. Fold thoroughly, but be gentle so you don't lose any of the incorporated air, which is the cake's only leavening.

Pour the batter into an ungreased 10-inch tube pan as evenly as possible. Cut through the batter with a spatula to remove any large air pockets. Lightly smooth the top of the batter.

Bake in a preheated oven for 30–40 minutes, or until the cake is brown and dry on top and springs back when you touch it lightly with your finger. Do not open the oven door for at least the first 20 minutes of baking.

When the cake is done, invert the pan on its legs or stand it on a funnel to cool upside down. Cool completely before removing from the pan. To remove, run a knife between the cake and the sides of the pan. Holding the pan upside down, push the bottom to separate the tube from the sides. Then remove the cake from the tube.

Serve plain with ice cream, topped with puréed fresh fruit, or iced with Seven-Minute Frosting (p. 146).

Unfrosted Angel Food Cake freezes very well if you cool completely before freezing.

Makes 1 10-inch cake.

Seven-Minute Frosting

> 2 egg whites
> 1½ cups granulated sugar
> ¼ teaspoon cream of tartar
> ⅓ cup cold water
> 1 teaspoon vanilla

Combine all the ingredients except vanilla in the top of a double boiler. Cook over boiling water, beating constantly with an electric mixer or hand-beater until the mixture forms soft peaks. This takes about 7 minutes. Remove from heat and beat in the vanilla. Continue beating until the frosting is the proper consistency for spreading.

Cake should be completely cool before frosting.

Makes enough frosting for a 10-inch angel food cake or a 9-inch 2-layer cake.

Strawberry Angel Cake

Try this for a super special occasion in June!

> 1 plain 10-inch Angel Food Cake (p. 145)
> ½ envelope unflavored gelatin
> 2 tablespoons cold water
> 1 cup heavy whipping cream
> ¼ cup granulated sugar (or more to taste)
> ¼ teaspoon almond extract
> ½ teaspoon vanilla extract
> 2 cups whole, hulled fresh strawberries

Working from the center, hollow out the cake, leaving a shell about 2 inches thick all the way around. (Freeze the chunks to serve with pudding or ice cream another day.)

Soften the gelatin in the water, then heat gently until the gelatin dissolves. Cool.

Begin beating the cream and gradually beat in the cooled gelatin. Whip the cream until it stands in peaks. Beat in the sugar and flavorings. Fold in all but about ½ cup of the strawberries. Pile the cream mixture into the hollowed-out cake. Garnish with the reserved berries and refrigerate for at least 1 hour before serving.

Makes 12 servings.

Holiday Chocolate Cake

This one-bowl cake gets its name because it's special enough for a holiday and so easy to make that it feels like one.

> 2 cups all-purpose flour
> 2 cups granulated sugar
> $3/4$ cup cocoa (not instant)
> 1 teaspoon baking powder
> 2 teaspoons baking soda
> 2 eggs
> 1 cup milk
> 1 cup hot coffee
> $1/2$ cup vegetable oil
> 1 teaspoon vanilla
> $1/2$ teaspoon ground cinammon

Preheat oven to 350°.

Add all ingredients in the order listed, without premixing or sifting anything. Mix as you add and pour the batter into two 9-inch cake pans or one oblong cake pan that has been greased and floured.

Bake for 30–40 minutes. Frost with Mocha Cream Frosting (below) when cool.

Makes a 9-inch double layer cake.

Mocha Cream Frosting

> 3 tablespoons soft butter
> 2 teaspoons milk
> 2 tablespoons strong hot coffee
> 3 tablespoons cocoa
> 2 cups powdered sugar
> $1/2$ teaspoon vanilla

In a medium bowl mix the butter, milk, and hot coffee. In a sifter combine the cocoa and powdered sugar and sift into the butter–cream mixture. Mix thoroughly. Add the vanilla. If the frosting seems too thick, thin it with tiny bits of milk; if it is too thick, sift in a little more sugar.

Southern Banana Cake

I make banana cake in cupcakes instead of a single large cake. The powdered sugar saves the frosting step. Banana cake freezes well.

$^1/_2$ cup butter
$1^1/_2$ cups brown sugar
2 eggs
1 cup mashed ripe banana
1 teaspoon lemon juice
1 teaspoon vanilla
2 cups flour
1 teaspoon baking powder
Pinch of salt
$^1/_2$ cup buttermilk
Powdered sugar

Preheat oven to 350°.

Cream butter and sugar. Add eggs and beat well. Add banana, lemon juice and vanilla. Combine flour, baking powder and salt, and add alternately with buttermilk to banana mixture. Beat well. Pour into greased and floured cake pan or cupcake pan.

Bake about 1 hour, or until cake tests done in the center, 50–60 minutes. Cupcakes require only about 30 minutes baking time.

Dust with powdered sugar while cake is still warm.

Makes 1 9-inch square cake or about 12 cupcakes.

York Gingerbread

That old, old favorite, gingerbread, deserves more attention than we give it these days, being sweet enough for dessert and light enough for breakfast or tea. It was often served at the Moravian Village of Salem, North Carolina.

> *6 teacups sugar, 3 butter, c molasses, 3 milk, 9 flour, 1 ginger, 6 eggs, 2 teaspoons of pearrlash dissolved in two table spoons of vinigar, 1 cup orange peel & spce. Bake in a loafe.*

That's the recipe as it appeared in the manuscript receipt collection of Louisa Senseman, the daughter of Salem silversmith John Volger.

Here is the adaptation that has been worked out by the domestic arts staff at the restored village, Old Salem, dividing the quantity in half and making the directions more specific, but keeping the same basic ingredients and proportions.

A special feature of this old recipe is that it calls for fresh ginger root, rather than powdered ginger. Don't substitute; the taste is significantly different.

> 1 cup + 2 tablespoons soft butter
> 2^1/$_4$ cups granulated sugar
> 3 eggs
> 1 cup + 2 tablespoons molasses
> ^{1}/$_4$ cup + 2 tablespoons peeled, sliced, and chopped *fresh* ginger root
> ^{1}/$_3$ cup grated orange peel (takes 2–3 oranges)
> 1 teaspoon ground cinnamon
> ^{1}/$_8$ teaspoon ground cloves
> 1 tablespoon vinegar
> 1 teaspoon baking soda
> 1 cup + 2 tablespoons milk
> 3^1/$_4$ cup + 2 tablespoons all-purpose flour

Preheat oven to 375°.

Cream together the butter and sugar. Add the eggs, beating after each addition. Mix in the molasses, ginger root, grated orange peel, cinnamon and cloves.

In a cup combine the vinegar and baking soda. Mix it into the batter. Alternately stir in the milk and flour, mixing after each addition.

Pour the batter into a greased and floured 9 × 13" pan. Bake 50–55 minutes or until done in the middle.

Gingerbread freezes well, but should not be kept more than about a week because the spices loose their zip. Serve hot or cold, plain or with lemon sauce or Chef's Sweet Whipped Cream (p. 151).

Simple Gingerbread

$^1/_3$ cup butter
$^2/_3$ cup hot coffee
1 cup molasses
$2^1/_4$ cups all-purpose flour
$1^1/_2$ teaspoons baking soda
$^1/_2$ teaspoon salt
1 teaspoon ground ginger
1 teaspoon ground cinnamon
$^1/_4$ teaspoon ground cloves

Preheat oven to 350°.

In a mixing bowl melt the butter into the hot coffee. Stir in the molasses. Sift the dry ingredients into the molasses mixture. Stir well.

Pour into a greased and floured 8-inch square pan, and bake for 25–30 minutes (or bake in muffin tins, reducing the baking time 5–10 minutes). Serve hot with Lemon Sauce (below) or Chef's Sweet Whipped Cream (p. 151). This gingerbread freezes well and is excellent reheated in the microwave.

Lemon Sauce

$^1/_3$ cup granulated sugar
1 tablespoon cornstarch
1 cup water
3 tablespoons butter
$^1/_2$ teaspoons grated lemon rind
$1^1/_2$ tablespoons fresh lemon juice

Combine the sugar and cornstarch in a saucepan. Stir in the water. Cook and stir over low heat until the sauce is clear and beginning to thicken. Remove from the heat and stir in the remaining ingredients. Serve warm.

Makes about $1^1/_4$ cups sauce.

Chef's Sweet Whipped Cream

Adding a small amount of unflavored gelatin to whipped cream helps it hold up much longer, so that you can whip the cream well ahead of time. I guess it would be sacrilege if you could get fine, unadulterated dairy cream dripping with butterfat and flavor, but given the relative blandness of grocery store cream, I don't mind helping it along a bit.

> 1 envelope unflavored gelatin
> 1/4 cup cold water
> 2 cups cold whipping cream
> 1/4–1/2 cup powdered sugar
> 1/2 teaspoon vanilla (optional)

Soften the gelatin in the water, then heat gently until the gelatin dissolves. Cool. In a large, chilled bowl begin beating the cream on low speed, gradually incorporating the gelatin. Beat on medium about 5 minutes, then increase speed to high and gradually beat in sugar and, if desired, vanilla.

To save extra whipped cream, place rosettes or dollops on a cookie sheet and freeze. Transfer the rosettes to a plastic bag. To serve later, arrange the frozen whipped cream where you want to use it and let it thaw in place.

Makes about 4 cups whipped cream.

Apples & Oranges Frozen Whip

A good time to make this is after you've prepared orange sherbet or ambrosia and have empty orange skins to use. It doesn't seem to make a great deal of difference in taste whether you use commercial or homemade applesauce in this recipe.

The dessert will keep in the freezer for several weeks. After the orange halves are frozen 1 hour as called for in the recipe, wrap them individually in plastic wrap and store in a freezer-weight plastic bag. To serve, unwrap and allow the orange halves to soften slightly.

> 1 egg white, at room temperature
> 2 tablespoons granulated sugar
> 2 teaspoons grated orange peel
> 1¼ cups applesauce
> 6 hollowed-out orange skin halves
> Cinnamon

Beat the egg white until frothy, then gradually add the sugar, about a teaspoon at a time, beating at high speed the entire time.

Beat in the grated orange peel. Continue beating until the egg white is glossy and forms stiff peaks, as for a soft meringue.

Thoroughly fold the applesauce into the egg white. Pile the mixture into the hollowed-out orange skins. Freeze for about 1 hour before serving.

Makes 6 servings.

Aunt Chloe's Charlotte Russe

One wonders about Aunt Chloe. This whipped cream concoction is liberally laced with spirits. Eating too much probably could knock you on your Sally Lunn buns.

> 2 envelopes unflavored gelatin
> 1 cup cold water
> 1 cup hot milk
> 4 cups whipping cream
> 5 tablespoons granulated sugar
> ½ cup bourbon
> ½ cup sherry
> 2 teaspoons vanilla

Soften the gelatin in cold water and add to hot milk. Cool. Whip cream with sugar until the cream stands in peaks. Beat in the bourbon, sherry and vanilla. Add gelatin and whip until the mixture starts to jell. Chill mixture. *This may be made a day ahead.* To serve, spoon into dessert dishes and serve with sponge cake or unfrosted Mother's Angel Food Cake (p. 145).

Orange Chiffon Pie with Coconut Shell

You need fresh, very sweet orange juice to make this pie best. Its flavor recalls those days when oranges were such a special treat that children looked forward to finding one in their Christmas stockings.

> 1 envelope unflavored gelatin
> 1/4 cup cold water
> 4 egg yolks
> 1/2 cup freshly squeezed orange juice
> 1/2 cup granulated sugar
> 1 teaspoon grated orange peel
> 4 egg whites at room temperature
> 1/2 cup granulated sugar
> 1 baked Coconut Pie Shell (below)
> 1 orange, thinly sliced

Soften the gelatin in the cold water.

Beat the egg yolks with the orange juice and 1/2 cup sugar. Cook the mixture in the top of a double boiler over (not in) boiling water until thick and smooth, 8–10 minutes. Remove from the heat.

Add the gelatin and stir until dissolved. Add the grated orange peel. Cool.

Beat the egg whites until foamy, then begin beating in the remaining 1/2 cup sugar, a spoonful at a time. When the whites are glossy and stand in peaks, as for meringue, fold them into the cooled orange custard mixture.

Pile the filling into the pie shell and chill for several hours or overnight. *This pie may be made a day ahead and kept in the refrigerator. Do not cover it.* Garnish with thin slices of fresh orange just before serving.

Coconut Pie Shell

Use this pie shell instead of pastry for any baked or chilled pie filling that holds its own shape when prepared. It's good, easy and light.

> Softened butter
> Granulated sugar
> 1 cup (6 ounces) shredded, sweetened coconut

Heavily butter a 9-inch pie plate. Sprinkle it with sugar. Firmly press the coconut against the sides and bottom of the plate.

For baked fillings, pour the mixture into the uncooked crust and proceed with baking.

For cold fillings, bake the empty shell in a preheated 375° oven for 10 minutes. Cook before filling.

Miss May's Crustless Cheesecake

What an inspired idea! Some pies, like this one, taste better without a thick crust, and not making crust saves time as well as calories. Using Neufchâtel and ricotta cheeses, instead of sour cream and cream cheese, and substituting skim milk for heavy cream cut a lot of the fat from this dessert without changing its divinely creamy consistency.

> Ground nuts or graham cracker crumbs
> 1 15-ounce container part skim ricotta cheese (a scant 2 cups)
> 2 8-ounce packages Neufchâtel cheese
> 1/2 cup evaporated skim milk
> 3 eggs
> 1/2 cup granulated sugar
> 1 teaspoon vanilla extract
> 2 tablespoons lemon juice
> 1 1/2 tablespoons cornstarch
> 2 tablespoons melted butter

Preheat oven to 400°.

Prepare a deep glass or pottery pie dish by buttering it heavily and dusting it with ground nuts or graham cracker crumbs.

In the blender or food processor, mix the cheeses, skim milk, eggs, sugar and vanilla.

Soften the cornstarch in the lemon juice. Add the cheese mixture along with the melted butter. Process until the mixture is completely smooth and creamy, scraping the sides of the processing container once or twice with a spatula.

Pour into the prepared pie dish.

Set the dish in a shallow pan of hot water. Bake for 10 minutes at 400°. Lower heat to 325° and bake about 30–40 minutes more. Remove from the oven before the center is fully firm. Cool in the hot-water bath. The cheesecake will finish setting as it cools.

You may make this cheesecake 3 or 4 days ahead and keep it, covered, in the refrigerator.

Serve with Raspberry–Orange Sauce (p. 155).

Makes 1 9-inch cheesecake.

Raspberry–Orange Sauce

This sauce will keep several weeks if tightly covered in the refrigerator.

> 2 6-ounce packages frozen raspberries
> 1 cup bitter orange marmalade

Defrost the raspberries. Drain the juice and reserve the berries for another use.

In a saucepan mix together the orange marmalade and raspberry juice.

Bring to a boil. Lower heat and simmer, stirring constantly, for 5–10 minutes, or until the mixture barely shows signs of thickening. It will thicken as it cools, taking about 24 hours.

Makes about 1½ cups sauce.

The Lightest Cheesecake

The base of this cheesecake is yogurt drained of its whey. Don't pass up the recipe just because you don't like yogurt. Once the whey is dripped out, the yogurt, which becomes very thick, loses its yogurt-ey taste.

To make drained yogurt you can either line a sieve with several layers of cheesecloth or use one of the dripping devices made expressly for the job. Either way, the yogurt should drain 24 hours. To know how much to start with, figure that it condenses to about half its original volume. If you have to make several batches, drained yogurt may be stored in a covered container until you have enough.

> Graham cracker crumbs
> 2 cups drained yogurt
> 1 teaspoon vanilla
> ¼ teaspoon lemon extract (optional)
> ¼ cup granulated sugar
> 2 eggs, lightly beaten
> 1 tablespoon cornstarch
> 1 7-inch crumb crust

Preheat oven to 325°.

Dust a 7-inch buttered pie pan heavily with crumbs.

Combine remaining ingredients and mix gently with a whisk or fork until well blended. To avoid lumps of cornstarch, it's a good idea to mix a small amount of egg or yogurt with the cornstarch until it thins out, then stir it into the rest of the mixture.

Bake 20–25 minutes. Cool and refrigerate uncovered 24 hours before serving.

Makes 6–8 servings.

Pumpkin Cookies

These cookies freeze beautifully. They're easy because they don't have to be rolled and cut. And they're nice after a heavy meal because they are fluffy and not too sweet.

You can use either canned pumpkin or homemade pumpkin purée. I find that canned pumpkin is one of the genuine bargains on the grocery-store shelves. It's inexpensive and consistently smooth and thick. Be sure to get pumpkin, *not* pumpkin pie mix.

> 5 cups all-purpose white flour
> 2 teaspoons baking soda
> 1 teaspoon salt
> 1 teaspoon ground cinnamon
> 1 teaspoon ground nutmeg
> 1 teaspoon ground cloves
> 2 cups butter or margarine
> 2 cups granulated sugar
> 3 eggs
> 2 cups pumpkin
> 3 teaspoons vanilla

Preheat oven to 350°.

Sift dry ingredients together. Cream butter and sugar. Blend in eggs, pumpkin and vanilla. Gradually add dry ingredients, mixing well. Drop batter from a teaspoon onto a greased cookie sheet. Bake about 10 minutes.

Makes about 12 dozen cookies.

Mama's Soft Sugar Cookies

To my taste, these are the best sugar cookies in the world. I've been eating them for almost half a century. No telling how many generations before loved them. They freeze perfectly, and my idea of heaven is a stock of several dozen in the freezer. The recipe doesn't make many, but it's better to mix up separate batches than to double the recipe.

> 1/2 cup granulated sugar
> 1/2 cup soft vegetable shortening
> 1 egg, beaten
> 1 3/4 cups sifted flour
> 1/4 teaspoon salt
> 1/2 teaspoon baking soda
> 2 teaspoons baking powder
> 1/4 cup milk
> 1/2 teaspoon lemon extract

Preheat oven to 400°.

Cream together the sugar, shortening and egg until fluffy. Sift together the flour, salt, baking soda and baking powder. Add the dry ingredients alternately with the milk and extract, beginning and ending with dry ingredients. Mix thoroughly. Chill the mixture 45 minutes.

To shape the cookies we used to roll the dough on a lightly floured board and cut with a large cutter, but it's quicker, easier and just as effective to form the dough into golf-ball sized pieces and flatten them on the cookie sheet with a glass bottom dipped in sugar. The cookies should not be less than 3/8-inch thick.

Bake at 400° for about 5 minutes. These cookies should not be brown. Cool on a rack before storing or serving.

Makes about 10 cookies.

Ice Cream, Sherbet, and Yogurt

Ice cream has always been a favorite Southern treat. Generally these recipes are lighter than standard ice cream recipes—a little less sweet, lower in fat. I tested all the recipes using the Waring Ice Cream Parlor. It is one of the electric ice-cream makers that uses ice cubes and table salt for freezing. Its maximum capacity is two quarts. The recipes could be made equally well in the ice-less units that you store in the freezer before making ice cream, provided you use one that is big enough.

The traditional final step in making ice cream is to remove the dasher and harden or mellow the ice cream by packing the canister in salt and ice. With today's ice-cream makers you can do it more simply by stirring the ice cream and packing it down with a wooden spoon right in the canister and then placing the canister in the freezer, or by putting the mixture into a plastic storage container in the freezer for a couple of hours. Personally, I like these desserts best while they are still soft frozen, in the dasher-licking stage. But they melt quickly at this point so if you decide to serve them straight from the churn, chill the serving dishes first and serve right away.

Remember that as they freeze, ice cream mixtures expand by a cup or more. Be sure to use a canister big enough to allow expansion room.

Vanilla Ice Cream

Make this with the freshest, highest quality cream you can find, preferably the kind without plastic preservatives to extend shelf life into the year 3000. The simple combination of flavors—sweet cream, plain vanilla and a touch of sugar—is glorious when it hits your tongue in a long, slow moment of cold and smooth melting. Heavy cream was once used without question, but light cream works just as well.

4 cups light cream
³/₄ cups granulated sugar
¹/₄ teaspoon salt
1 tablespoon vanilla extract

Bring the cream almost to a boil then remove from the heat and stir in the sugar and salt.

When the sugar is dissolved, refrigerate the mixture until it is cold.

Stir in the vanilla. and pour into the freezing canister of an ice-cream maker and freeze according to the directions for the appliance. Serve immediately, or harden in the freezing canister packed in ice or in a plastic storage container in your freezer.

Makes about 6 cups, enough for 6–8 servings.

Orange Sherbet

The better the orange juice you use, the better the sherbet will be. Don't worry if the mixture curdles; it will smooth out as it freezes.

1 cup freshly squeezed orange juice
¹/₂ cup lemon juice
1 cup granulated sugar
2 cups milk
¹/₄ teaspoon salt
1 teaspoon vanilla extract

Mix together the orange and lemon juices and the sugar, stirring until the sugar has dissolved.

Add the milk, salt and vanilla and beat well.

Pour into the freezing canister of an ice-cream maker and freeze according to the directions for the appliance. Serve immediately, or harden in the freezing canister packed in ice or in a plastic storage container in your freezer.

Makes about 4 cups, enough for 4–6 servings.

Blackberry–Orange Parfait

For each serving:

> 2 small scoops Orange Sherbet (p. 159)
> 1 ounce blackberry brandy
> $1/4$ cup red or black raspberries

Put the sherbet into a tall-stemmed glass. Drizzle the brandy over the sherbet and top with the berries. Serve at once.

Cantaloupe Sherbet

An elegant dessert. Don't worry about the cup of heavy cream; when mixed with the other ingredients it becomes a relatively small part of the total volume. If you eat one serving of sherbet, you get only $1/12$ of a cup (a little over a tablespoon) of cream.

> $1^1/4$ cups milk
> 1 cup granulated sugar
> 1 completely ripe cantaloupe
> $1/3$ cup lemon juice
> 1 cup whipping cream
> 2 egg whites, at room temperature

Bring the milk almost to a boil. Remove from the heat and add the sugar, stirring until it is dissolved. Refrigerate.

While the mixture is chilling, scoop out the flesh of the cantaloupe and purée in a blender or food processor. Add the purée and lemon juice to the milk.

Whip the cream and fold it in. Beat the egg whites until stiff and fold in.

Pour into the freezing canister of an ice-cream maker and freeze according to the directions for the appliance. Harden in the freezing canister packed in ice or in a plastic storage container in your freezer.

Makes about 8 cups, or enough for 8–12 servings.

Quick Strawberry Ice Cream

It doesn't need an ice-cream freezer!

I didn't expect much from this recipe when I tried it, but the ice cream is surprisingly good, definitely superior to packaged ice cream, and embarrassingly easy. You need a blender or food processor to make it.

> 3 cups whole frozen strawberries
> 1/2 cup whipping cream
> 2 eggs
> 1/3 cup granulated sugar
> 2 teaspoons lemon juice
> 1/2 teaspoon vanilla

Soften the berries a few minutes before beginning.

Mix the cream, eggs and sugar in the blender or food processor. Turn the machine on and off quickly, processing just enough to mix the ingredients.

With the motor running, feed in the frozen strawberries one at a time. Blend or process until the mixture is smooth, stopping to stir with a spatula if necessary. Add the lemon juice and vanilla in the last few seconds of processing.

Serve at once or store in your freezer. If you store the ice cream in the freezer, remove it about 15 minutes before serving to soften it slightly.

Makes about 4 servings. (To double the recipe, prepare in two batches.)

Strawberry Sherbet

The flavor of this sherbet is intense. The better and sweeter the strawberries you use, the more delicious the sherbet.

About 3 cups fresh whole strawberries
1 envelope unflavored gelatin
1/4 cup cold water
1/2 cup orange juice
1/4–1/2 cup granulated sugar (to taste)
1 cup whipping cream

Wash and hull the strawberries. Purée them in a blender or food processor.

Soften the gelatin in the cold water.

Bring the orange juice just to a boil and dissolve the softened gelatin in it. Allow the mixture to cool, then combine it with the puréed strawberries.

Taste. This sherbet depends on the strawberries and orange juice for its sweetness. If the sherbet is not sweet enough, dissolve 1/4–1/2 cup sugar in the hot orange juice, but be careful because the sherbet should not be so sweet it overpowers the strawberry flavor.

Whip the cream and fold it in. Pour into the freezing canister of an ice-cream maker and freeze according to the directions for the appliance. Serve immediately, or harden in the freezing canister packed in ice or in a plastic storage container in your freezer.

Makes about 6 cups, enough for 6–8 servings.

Mixed Fruit Sherbet

Here is a smooth, mellow frozen dessert that tastes rich without using a speck of cream. Mixing it in a food processor makes it a quick and easy recipe.

2 ripe medium-sized bananas
²/₃ cup granulated sugar
¹/₂ teaspoon grated lemon peel
¹/₃ cup orange juice
1 tablespoon lemon juice
1 cup cranberry juice cocktail
1 egg white, at room temperature

Mash the bananas.

Work in the sugar, lemon peel and juices. Process until the mixture is smooth.

Beat the egg white until stiff. Fold into the fruit mixture.

Pour into the freezing container of an ice-cream maker and freeze according to directions for the appliance. Serve at once—no additional hardening needed.

Makes about 4 cups, enough for 4–6 servings.

Lemon Ice

3 lemons
¹/₂ cup granulated sugar
2 cups water
Lemon twists for garnish

Pare off the zest (yellow part) of the lemon rinds with a sharp knife or vegetable peeler. Squeeze the lemons and set the juice aside.

Heat the sugar and water in a saucepan with the lemon zest until the sugar is dissolved. Bring to a boil, and boil for 5 minutes. Remove from the heat, add the lemon juice, cool and strain. Chill for at least 30 minutes.

Pour into the freezing canister of an ice-cream maker and freeze according to the directions for the appliance. Harden in the freezing canister packed in ice or in a plastic storage container in your freezer.

Serve garnished with lemon twists.

Frozen Raspberry Yogurt

If you don't like yogurt, give this a try anyway because it doesn't taste at all "yogurt-ey"—just smooth and creamy. You can prepare the base in minutes with a food processor or blender.

8-ounce package frozen raspberries
1 cup plain yogurt
1 envelope unflavored gelatin
3 tablespoons cold water
2 egg whites, at room temperature
1/3 cup granulated sugar

Thaw the raspberries and process in the blender or food processor until smooth. Strain out the seeds and return to processor bowl.

Mix in the yogurt and process briefly.

Soften the gelatin in the cold water, then dissolve over low heat. Add to the raspberry mixture and process again for a few seconds.

In a large bowl, beat the egg whites until stiff, then gradually beat in the sugar. Continue beating until you feel no grittiness when you rub a bit of the meringue mixture between your fingers.

Fold the purée into the meringue. Pour into the freezing canister of an ice-cream maker and freeze according to the directions for the appliance. Serve immediately, or harden in the freezing canister packed in ice or in a plastic storage container in your freezer.

Makes about 6 cups, enough for 6–8 servings.

Frozen Peach Yogurt

To my taste, this frozen yogurt is refreshingly tangy. If you have a pro-
nounced sweet tooth, you may want to use a bit more sugar than the recipe
requires. Use very ripe peaches.

> 3–4 fresh medium-sized peaches
> 1/3 cup granulated sugar
> 1 tablespoon lemon juice
> 1 envelope unflavored gelatin
> 1/4 cup water
> 3 cups plain yogurt
> 1 teaspoon vanilla extract
> 1/4 teaspoon almond extract

Peel and cut up the peaches. Purée them in a blender or food processor
with the sugar and lemon juice. Set aside.

Soften the gelatin in the cold water, then warm it over low heat until the
gelatin dissolves. Cool and add to the peaches.

Add the yogurt and flavorings and process until well mixed and
smooth.

Pour the yogurt mixture into the freezing canister of an ice-cream maker
and freeze according to the directions for the appliance. Serve immediately,
or harden in the freezing canister packed in ice or in a plastic storage container in your freezer.

BEVERAGES

Beverages With Spirit

Mint Julep

Some Southerners argue as passionately about the best way to make a mint julep as football fans do about quarterbacks. If you haven't a favorite of your own, this recipe produces a good, easy-to-manage drink.

Fill tall glasses or metal julep cups with chopped ice (you can use the blender or food processor to chop it) and keep the glasses in the freezer until serving time.

Keep a bouquet of fresh mint in water in the refrigerator.

For each drink measure 2 teaspoons simple syrup and 2 ounces (¼ cup) good bourbon into a mixing jar. Add a few sprigs of mint. Stir vigorously. Don't worry about bruising the mint. This may be done ahead of time and held, covered, at room temperature until serving time.

To serve, remove the glasses of ice from the freezer. Take the mint out of the bourbon. Gradually pour the bourbon into the glasses, stirring gently to help the ice melt slightly. Garnish each glass with fresh mint and serve at once with long straws.

Whiskey Sour

> 1 6-ounce can lemonade concentrate
> 6 ounces water
> 6 ounces whiskey
> ½–1 teaspoon powdered sugar
> Cracked ice

Pour lemonade (still frozen) into blender jar or food processor along with the water, whiskey and powdered sugar. Cover and process on high, adding ice cubes or ice a little at a time, until mixture is slushy. Serve immediately.

Makes 6–8 servings.

Peach Daiquiri

Make Peach Daiquiris only when you have beautiful, fresh peaches. Because the drinks should be made in small batches and served immediately, peach daiquiris aren't practical for more than about six people.

You need either a blender or a food processor for this recipe. If you use a food processor, you can prepare two batches at a time.

1 medium-sized fresh ripe peach
1 tablespoon fresh lime juice
2 teaspoons granulated sugar
6 tablespoons white rum
1 cup cracked ice

Peel the peach and cut it into quarters. Put it into the blender with the lime juice, sugar and rum. Cover the blender and process at high speed. Add the ice, a little at a time, processing continuously. When the mixture is thick and slushy, pour into large cocktail glasses and serve at once.

Makes 2–3 servings.

Strawberry Daiquiri

You'll find this daiquiri recipe a little less trouble than the Peach Daiquiri, and a little sweeter, too. If you use frozen strawberries, you can serve it in any season. Use a blender or food processor. If you use a blender, you'll have beter results by dividing the recipe in half and making the drinks in two batches.

1 16-ounce bag of whole, unsweetened, frozen strawberries
1/2 cup cream of coconut
1/4 cup lemon juice
1/4 cup grenadine syrup
1 1/2 cups light rum
1/2–1 cup cracked ice

Do not thaw the strawberries. Purée them in the blender or food processor. Add the remaining ingredients and process until smooth. Serve at once in large cocktail glasses.

Makes 4–5 servings.

Southern Eggnog

To make eggnog for a crowd, try this recipe, typical of old Southern recipes, but with at least a bit of the fat and cholesterol cut. It's an adaptation of the classic recipe John Egerton offers in his book, *Southern Food*. The best way to make this is with an electric mixer.

> 12 eggs, separated
> 1 cup powdered sugar
> 2–4 cups bourbon (to taste)
> 1/3 cup light rum
> 2 cups half-and-half
> 2 cups milk
> 2 cups whipping cream
> Nutmeg

Combine the egg yolks and sugar in a mixing bowl and beat until the sugar dissolves and mixture is foamy. Beat in the bourbon, rum, half-and-half and milk. (Or use all cream if you're feeling totally decadent!)

In a separate bowl, whip the heavy cream until it stands in soft peaks. Beat the egg whites until they stand in soft peaks. Fold the whipped cream and egg whites into the bourbon mixture. Pour into a gallon jar (commercial mayonnaise jars are the right size and work well) and refrigerate two or three days before serving.

At serving time, pour into a chilled punch bowl and grate a generous amount of nutmeg over the top.

Makes a little less than a gallon, about 25 servings.

Eggnog for a Few Friends

This version is less rich and fluffy, but good. It, too, tastes better if it is refrigerated for a day or two before serving.

> 4 eggs, separated
> 1/4 cup powdered sugar
> 1 cup half-and-half
> 1/2–1 cup bourbon (to taste)
> 1/4 cup light rum (optional)
> Vanilla (optional)
> Nutmeg

Beat the egg yolks and sugar together until the sugar dissolves and the mixture is foamy. Beat in the half-and-half and liquors.

In a separate bowl, whip the egg whites until they stand in soft peaks. Whip in a few drops of vanilla, if you wish, for a richer taste. Fold the egg whites into the bourbon mixture.

Pour the eggnog into two quart jars and refrigerate at least a day. Shake before serving. To serve, pour the eggnog into individual cups and grate nutmeg over top.

Make 6 to 8 servings.

Savannah Punch

Savannah's most famous punch is Chatham Artillery Punch, a concoction with which residents allegedly entertained scores of visiting dignitaries and military men, including President Monroe. The list of ingredients reads like a late-night fraternity party desperation punch, calling as it does for tea, wine, rum, brandy, gin, rye and champagne. The results taste mellow, but the effects on the imbiber are absolutely lethal—not the sort of thing a hostess can serve in good conscience. The following recipe is for a more reasonable, still mellow punch.

> 3/4 cup light honey
> 6 cups hot strong tea
> 2 cups orange juice
> 1 cup lemon juice
> 3 cups Southern Comfort
> 1 quart club soda
> 1 fifth champagne

Dissolve the honey in the tea. Cool and mix with the orange and lemon juices. Chill.

At serving time, put ice into the punch bowl and pour in the tea–juice mixture, Southern Comfort, club soda and champagne.

Makes 5 quarts, about 30 servings.

Champagne Cooler

This is really a variation on mimosa, the popular mixture of champagne and orange juice. Champagne Coolers are easy to prepare in a pitcher for a few people or in a punch bowl for a larger group.

> 1 6-ounce can frozen grapefruit juice concentrate, thawed
> 4 teaspoons grenadine
> 3 cups champagne

Mix the juice and grenadine in a pitcher. Just before serving, pour in the champagne.

Makes 6 servings.

Strawberry–Champagne Punch

For a stronger punch use a second bottle of champagne instead of the ginger ale, or spike it with vodka.

> 1 6-ounce package frozen sliced strawberries
> 1 6-ounce can frozen lemonade concentrate
> 1 6-ounce can frozen orange juice concentrate
> 1 quart soda water
> 1 fifth dry champagne
> Thinly sliced lemons for garnish

Partly thaw the strawberries and combine them in a punch bowl with the frozen lemonade and orange juice concentrates. Allow the ingredients to stand about half an hour, or longer, in the refrigerator. Just before serving, add soda water and champagne and ice or ice ring. Garnish with lemon slices.

Makes about 3 quarts, enough for 20 servings.

Nonalcoholic Beverages

Old-Fashioned Lemonade

Most of us have been drinking instant and frozen lemonade for so long we've forgotten how truly delicious the real thing is.

Don't be tempted to substitute bottled or frozen lemon juice for fresh lemons. The taste is different. Old-timers say to get the best flavor, you should have the lemons at room temperature and you should roll them under your hand with firm pressure against a countertop before squeezing.

> 1 cup granulated sugar
> 1 cup water
> 1 cup fresh lemon juice
> 5 cups water
> Mint or lemon slices for garnish

Boil the 1 cup sugar and 1 cup water together, stirring, until the sugar dissolves. Chill. Combine this syrup with the lemon juice and the rest of the water. Serve over ice cubes in tall glasses, garnished with mint, or if you can't find that, thin slices of lemon.

Makes 2 quarts, about 10 servings.

> *Variations*
> - Old-Fashioned Limeade: Substitute
>   3/4 cup fresh lime juice for lemon juice.
> - Old-Fashioned Orangeade: Substitute
>   2 cups of orange juice for lemon juice,
>   reduce sugar 3/4 cup and increase water
>   to 6 cups.

Grapefruit Spritzer

1 6-ounce can frozen grapefruit juice concentrate
2¹/₄ cups chilled club soda
4 teaspoons grenadine

Thaw the grapefruit juice and pour it, undiluted, into a pitcher. Gently mix in the club soda. To serve, pour 1 teaspoon of grenadine into the bottom of each of 4 glasses, drop in ice cubes, and fill with grapefruit mixture.

Makes 4 servings.

Pineapple–Mint Fizz

Cracked ice
2 cups pineapple juice
4 tablespoons fresh lime juice
Club soda
Fresh mint

Fill 4 tall glasses with ice and keep the glasses in the freezer until serving time.

Mix pineapple juice and lime juice. This may be done ahead of time and held, covered, in the refrigerator until serving time.

To serve, remove the glasses of ice from the freezer. Gradually pour the lime–pineapple juice into the glasses, filling about three-fourths full. Stir to mix ice and juices. Finish filling the glasses with club soda. Stir gently and garnish with fresh mint. Serve at once with long straws.

Makes 4 servings.

Lemon–Grape Fizz

¹/₄ cup Lemon Ice (p. 163) or commercial lemon sorbet
¹/₂ cup red (not purple) grape juice
Club soda

Spoon the lemon ice into the bottom of a tall glass. Pour the grape juice over it and stir to soften slightly. Fill the glass with club soda and stir just enough to mix. Serve with a straw.

Makes 1 serving.

Fruit Punch

1 6-ounce can frozen limeade concentrate
1 6-ounce can frozen orange juice concentrate
4 cups water
⅓ cup grenadine

Thaw the concentrates, mix with the water and grenadine and serve over ice in tall frosted glasses.

Makes 6 servings.

Pineapple–Lime Punch

4 cups granulated sugar
4 cups water
1 cup lime juice
8 cups unsweetened pineapple juice (made from frozen concentrate is best)
8 cups club soda
Mint for garnish

Boil together the sugar and water until the sugar is dissolved. Chill. Mix with the lime juice and pineapple juice. At serving time pour into a punch bowl with ice, add the club soda and garnish with mint.

Makes 5 quarts, about 30 servings.

Dessert Coffees

Coffee beverages let you linger at the end of a meal with a dessert feeling, perfect when you're plenty full already and simply want to extend the dinner-table ambiance for a while. It's too bad we don't do more with coffee drinks. The possibilities extend far beyond the familiar Irish Coffee and espresso. Below are some suggestions for coffee–liqueur–garnish combinations. In thinking up more of your own, remember that you want to mix complimentary flavors for interesting contrasts.

When you're using coffee drinks for desserts, it's worth going beyond your standard brand to use some of the more unusual kinds of coffee beans available in department stores and gourmet shops or by mail from gourmet catalogs. You can buy them ground, but I think the added intensity of flavor you get from freshly ground beans is worth the trouble. Unground beans keep well in the freezer for several weeks. The food writer, Karen Hess, goes so far as to buy green beans and roast her own (in an electric hot-air corn popper, no less) because she knows that roasted beans don't stay fresh indefinitely.

Serve your coffee combinations in thin cups. Encourage guests to try it first without cream and sugar even if they usually add those things.

Coffee with Amaretto and Cognac

1 cup French Roast coffee
1 ounce Amaretto & Cognac liqueur (or $1/2$ ounce each of
    Amaretto and Cognac)
Garnish with shaved toasted almonds

Coffee with Grand Marnier

1 cup Colombian coffee
1 ounce Grand Marnier
Garnish with twist of orange peel

Irish Mist Coffee

1 cup Colombian coffee
1 ounce Irish Mist
Garnish with small spoon of whipped cream

Comfort and Coffee

1 cup coffee with chicory
1 ounce Southern Comfort
Garnish with lemon twist

Chocolate Mint Coffee

1 cup mocha-java coffee
1 ounce chocolate-mint liqueur
Garnish with shaved bitter chocolate

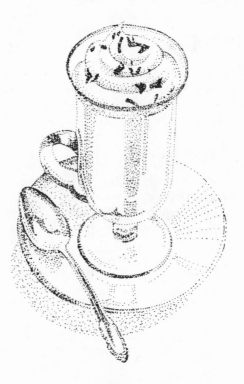

Apricot Coffee

> 1 cup Kona coffee
> 1 ounce apricot brandy
> Garnish with cinnamon stick

Kahlua Mocha Coffee

> 1 cup mocha-java coffee
> 1 ounce Kahlua
> 1 ounce milk
> Garnish heavily with shaved milk chocolate

Italian Coffee

> 1 cup dark Amaretto roast coffee
> 1 ounce Amaretto
> Garnish with vanilla ice cream

Chocolate Coffee

> 1 cup Swiss chocolate almond roast coffee
> 1 ounce Swiss chocolate almond liqueur
> Garnish with shaved Swiss chocolate

Coffee and Cognac

> 1 cup Kopenhagen coffee
> 1 ounce Cognac
> Garnish with twist of lemon peel

4

Appendices

ABOUT INGREDIENTS

Too often we confuse good food with *fancy* or *exotic* food. As imported ingredients and international recipes have become increasingly popular, we have begun to act as if food that is unusual or comes from far away—kiwi fruit or abalone, for instance—is elegant, while traditional and familiar foods like pork or potatoes are too plain for party fare.

But that is not the Southern way. Everyone who eats Southern cooking—and everyone who talks or writes about it—celebrates its use of traditional and seasonal foods—the freshest and best quality. Unfortunately, as anyone knows who has tasted a supermarket tomato lately, unless you have a garden it's a lot easier to get kiwi fruit and abalone than it is to get fresh, high quality, unadulterated ingredients to cook with.

The best Southern cooking has, historically, been supported by a garden, a hen house, fresh game and seafood and lots of pork. Well, today the pork at least is no problem. Miraculously enough, in recent years pork has become less fatty and more readily available without losing its flavor. But it's worth your life to find chicken that tastes like chicken; fresh, frozen or canned vegetables that taste like anything at all; or seafood that hasn't been around long enough to draw Social Security.

The problems come not only from commercial processing but also from hybridizing for faster growth, better shipping quality, and sometimes even better appearance. This isn't just a curmudgeon speaking: I had an opportunity to meet Edna Lewis, an award-winning Southern cook, notable not only because she carried her expertise to New York, but also because she has been willing to share her Southern recipes and cooking secrets through magazine articles and books.

The summer I talked with her, Edna Lewis was cooking at the restaurant at Middleton Plantation in Charleston, South Carolina. Upon discovering that we both had an interest in organic gardening and growing non-hybridized, old-fashioned vegetables, she told me that she was working on a book called *In Pursuit of Flavor,* dealing with just such things. I learned that she was a gardener who did more than complain that hybrids had less flavor; she was one who deliberately set about growing old-timey vegetables for their superior taste.

She talked, also, about the subtleties of baking, of how she'd had to abandon a large amount of flour mistakenly ordered for the restaurant because it wasn't the right kind to make good biscuits.

We also talked about what makes good ice cream (good cream, of course) and other culinary matters for almost an hour.

When I ordered dinner, I asked many questions about what was best on the menu, and each time the message from Edna in the kitchen was to choose what was fresh, seasonal and newly prepared.

That's the ideal.

A person could die trying to live up to it.

As I discussed in my preface, it's the labor dilemma again. One Tennessee family I know used to maintain a beautiful garden producing baskets and bushels of produce, enough to put up for winter and eat in season, with lots of okra, tomatoes, peppers, and squash left over for giving away. They did it without gardeners. They had six kids whose routine chores included a lot of planting, hoeing and picking. These days, we don't have gardeners and most of us don't even have six kids. Or space for much of a garden.

But look how it was in the old times. This description, written in October 1877, comes from *The Letters and Diary of Laura M. Towne:*

> My vegetable garden is fine; such growing I never saw.
> We have green peas, lettuce, cocoas, lima beans, egg-
> plant, spinach, and onions in use, and coming on, a
> splendid lot of cabbages, cauliflowers, carrots, beets, sal-
> sify, turnips. and later peas. The dear little "Tom
> Thumbs" were planted about the middle of September,
> and are just now beating nicely. I shall never fail to have a
> plentiful supply.

And in May 1869, William Gilmore Simms included this observation in a letter to Paul Hamilton Hayne in May 1869:

> I have probably the finest garden in all this precinct. I
> have set out 1200 cabbage plants, have been eating rad-
> ishes, lettuces, green peas, snapbeans & have squashes
> beginning to bear, corn in tassel, beans in any quantity,
> sweet corn for the table, tomato, cucumber, Irish potatoes,
> okra, onions, white & red eschalots, turnips, beets, car-
> rots, parsnips, and most of the herbs…I hope with these
> vegetable supplies, a little meat will suffice.

We have to compensate, fake it, make do. If you have the possibility of a small garden, grow those vegetables that taste best fresh and are hard to buy. If everyone around you grows enough tomatoes and squash to give away, you could concentrate on cucumbers, okra, and so on.

If you garden and would like to try growing some vegetable varieties specifically bred for flavor rather than glamorous appearance or shipping quality, you may be interested in experimenting with some seeds that aren't sold through the major catalogs. I've had good luck with Shepherd's Garden Seeds. In addition to concentrating on table vegetables rather than commercial varieties, they've begun a special line of seeds specifically for container gardening, so that even on an apartment balcony it's possible that you could grow enough cucumbers or tomatoes to steal the show at a dinner party.

If even a small garden is impossible, try to figure out some way to grow parsley, thyme, and dill, if nothing else. These fresh herbs change the taste of what you cook so much that even people with lead palates notice.

Farmers' markets are a good source of fruits and vegetables that taste real. The smaller markets are less expensive than big ones and the produce is apt to be better.

Another more expensive option is to buy some produce from natural-foods stores offering organically raised fruits and vegetables. One taste will tell you whether or not the goods you buy this way are worth the money and effort. I've found that if the store is a good one I can taste the difference immediately.

If you have no alternative to the supermarket, shop at one noted for keeping a good produce counter. Some foods are quite acceptable: cabbage, onions, celery, greens, sweet potatoes and white potatoes, for example. With peppers, squash, eggplant and cucumbers you'll probably have mixed results. Tomatoes are hopeless.

Some frozen foods taste pretty good, too. I've had luck with green peas, chopped spinach, creamed corn, brussels sprouts, and limas. A frozen "Southern Collection"—including butter peas, butter beans, field peas and snaps, blackeyes, and chopped turnip greens—is surprisingly good. I like the frozen chopped collards, too. Frozen okra can't pass for fresh, but will suffice in gumbos.

Then there are flours and cornmeal. Grocery store soft biscuit flour is fine. The whole-grain flours lack flavor because they've been de-germinated to prolong shelf life. If you can get cornmeal and grits that are produced in the region, they'll be good because they're fresher.

As for poultry and dairy products, if you can find a local dairy that sells milk and cream that hasn't been treated to prolong shelf life, you'll love the flavor. Whether or not you should be using cream and whole milk is another matter, but it's no worse for you than the non-dairy substitutes containing palm oil, an ingredient loaded with cholesterol. I use unsalted butter because I like the taste, but I always feel a little guilty about it. I don't know what to think about the nutritional characteristics of corn oil margarines, but since so many people these days have been urged to use them by their doctors, I have tested all the recipes in this book using both margarine and butter. In most cases it makes little difference which you use. In those few recipes where only butter will work, I've said so.

What about convenience foods? I think some of them are OK. Instant grits, for example, seem to taste about the same as long- cooking grits, expecially if you're using them combined with other ingredients. It seems to me you should use any convenience food that tastes right to you with no apologies. The problem with convenience foods, generally, is that nearly everybody is using them every day, so when you encounter them at a party they don't seem special. And that, also, isn't the Southern way.

MANAGING
LARGE
GROUPS

Until rather recently, books on entertaining included instructions for figuring how many kitchen helpers, waiters, and bartenders you needed for the size group you were planning to entertain. The modern, realistic version of this is "Get all the help you can." That help will probably consist of an offspring, a best friend and a spouse—if you're lucky.

In the absence of an optimum number of helpers, the advice to do everything possible well ahead of time becomes more important than ever. Your freezer replaces a kitchen helper, bowls or pitchers of punch replace the bartender, and buffet service replaces waiters. Beyond that, a surprising number of little practices can make it easier than you'd imagine possible to entertain many people. Some of the tricks speed up preparation; some simplify service. When you start thinking this way, you discover that almost everything you do could be managed more simply. In school we used to call it the KISS theory of entertaining. KISS means "Keep It Simple, Stupid." Here's my list of simplifiers. I know once you start thinking this way you'll be able to extend the list to fit your own situation.

- Above all else, send invitations and ask for RSVPs. You need to know how many people are coming so that you're not worried about whether you have enough food and you're not stuck scrambling at the last minute because more people came than you expected. Believe me, it happens. A lot.

- Don't become an assembly-line worker. Avoid foods that require a lot of individual assembly. For example, don't serve individual canapés and such pretty-but-time-consuming appetizers as stuffed mushrooms, stuffed cherry tomatoes, bacon-wrapped tidbits, and shrimp that take forever to shell. Rely instead on sliced cheese and meat and spreads, molds and dips to be spread by the guests on thinly sliced breads and good crackers.

- Use individual-sized baked goods where you can. That may sound as though it contradicts the previous point, but it doesn't really. On a buffet, slicing bread gets messy and slows down movement; cutting fancy cakes or pies requires almost constant attention. If you cut these items ahead of time and set them out on plates, they get stale and you have to keep bringing in more plates. Moreover, individual portions are easy to make ahead and freeze so that you can bring out only what you need. Most cake recipes bake up beautifully in muffin tins. Cookies are easy to make, easy to store, easy to serve, and easy to eat. Rolls, biscuits, and muffins look and work better on the buffet than whole loaves of bread.

■ Avoid spending a lot of time on fancy garnishes, elaborate-looking desserts and intricately frosted cakes. Those are the characteristics of a catered party, not home entertainment. If you're skeptical about the value of this advice, make a few radish roses and carrot curls and flute a few mushrooms and see how much time it takes. Garnishing is important but there are simpler ways of doing it, as I've suggested in the menu and recipes sections. Remember, this stuff is for people to eat. It should taste wonderful and look attractive, but it doesn't have to be museum-art quality.

■ Supplement your own cooking with purchased items. If you really want a fancy cake maybe you should order it. Commercial pâtés make excellent appetizers, as do several commercial whole-wheat and sesame crackers are excellent.

Have a delicatessen roast and slice meat or cut cheese for you. Then you can arrange it your way on your own platters, so it doesn't look catered.

■ Serve some foods that are good at room temperature or need to be cool but not frozen. The rule about keeping hot foods hot and cold foods cold is right, but it's a lot of work. The more forgiving foods don't require as much attention.

■ Avoid the bartender syndrome. If you start making one drink at a time, you'll spend all your time making drinks. I like punch in pitchers even better than in bowls because it doesn't have to be ladled and you can keep extra pitchers full and ready in the refrigerator.

■ Keep your decorations simple. Florists' centerpieces not only require money to buy and time to order, they also demand extra attention. Where should you put them? How can you protect them? Use what's available near your house that will look lovely with a minimum of arranging. A vase of wildflowers, a pitcher of fall leaves, a crock filled with evergreen branches cut from hedges— all these surprise and delight guests. Of course I'm not suggesting that if you live next door to the White House you should borrow flowers from the Rose Garden, but you get the idea.

■ Use wash-and-wear linens and dishwasher-safe dinnerware.

■ Wear clothing that can't be ruined by spills and shoes that don't hurt your feet. I'm not kidding. You're having this party for fun, remember? If it's an obligation of some kind, have it catered and don't think of it as a party at all.

BOOKS TO
READ ALOUD

The Best Loved Poems of the American People, edited by Hazel Felleman. Doubleday, New York.

Coastal Ghosts, by Nancy Rhyne. The East Woods Press, Charlotte.

Dixie Ghosts, edited by Frank D. McSherry, Jr., Charles G. Waugh and Martin H. Greenberg. Rutledge Hill Press, Nashville.

Favorite Scary Stories of American Children, collected by Richard and Judy Dockrey Young. August House, Little Rock.

Ghost Stories from the American South, compiled and edited by W.K.McNeil. August House, Little Rock.

Ghosts and Spectres of the Old South, by Nancy Roberts. Sandlapper Press, Greenville, South Carolina.

The Jack Tales: Folk Tales from the Southern Appalachians, collected and retold by Richard Chase. Houghton-Mifflin, New York.

A Modern Southern Reader, edited by Ben Forkner and P. Samway. Peachtree Publishers, Atlanta.

My Health is Better in November: 35 Stories of Hunting and Fishing in the South, by Havilah Babcock. University of South Carolina Press, Columbia.

Nightmares in Dixie: Thirteen Horror Tales from the American South, edited by Frank D. McSherry, Jr., Charles G. Waugh and Martin H. Greenberg. August House, Little Rock.

BIBLIOGRAPHY

Brown, Marion. *Southern Cook Book*. Rev. ed. Chapel Hill: University of North Carolina Press, 1968.

Bryan, Lettice. *The Kentucky Housewife*. Cincinnati: Shepard & Stearnes, 1839.

Butler, Cleora. *Cleora's Kitchens, the Memoir of a Cook*. Tulsa: Council Oak Books, Ltd., 1985.

Chesnut, Mary. *Mary Chesnut's Civil War Diary*. Edited by C. Vann Woodward. New Haven: Yale University Press, 1981.

Devereux, Catherine Ann. *Journal of a Secesh Lady*. Edited by Beth Gilbert Crabtree and James W. Patton. Raleigh: North Carolina Division of Archives and History, 1979.

Edgerton, Clyde. *Raney*. Chapel Hill, North Carolina: Algonquin Books, 1985.

Egerton, John. *Southern Food*. New York: Alfred A. Knopf, Inc., 1987.

Two Hundred Years of Charleston Cooking. Rev. ed. Columbia: University of South Carolina Press, 1976.

Hilliard, Sam Bowers. *Hog Meat and Hoecake*. Carbondale: Southern Illinois University Press, 1972.

Horry, Harriott Pinckney. *A Colonial Plantation Cookbook: The Receipt Book of Harriott Pinckney Horry, 1770*. Edited by Richard J. Hooker. Columbia: University of South Carolina Press, 1984.

Ingraham, J.H., ed. *The Sunny South or the Southerner at Home*. Philadelphia: G.G. Evans Publishers, 1860.

Kuehnle, Rob. "On Being Southern." *Mississippi*, May–June 1985.

Lambert, Walter. *Kinfolks and Custard Pie: Recollections and Recipes from an East Tennessean*. Knoxville: University of Tennessee Press, 1988.

Lewis, Edna. *The Taste of Country Cooking*. New York: Alfred A. Knopf, Inc., 1976.

McCulloch-Williams, Martha. *Dishes & Beverages of the Old South*. 1913. Reprint, Knoxville: University of Tennessee Press, 1988.

Sibley, Celestine. *A Place Called Sweet Apple*. 1967. Reprint, Atlanta: Peachtree Publishers, 1985.

Simms, William Gilmore. *The Letters of William Gilmore Simms* Vol. V. Edited by Mary C. Simms Oliphant and T.C. Duncan Eaves. Columbia: University of South Carolina Press, 1982.

Towne, Laura M. *The Letters and Diary of Laura M. Towne*. Edited by Rupert Sargent Holland. New York: Negro Universities Press, 1969.

Wecter, Dixon. *The Saga of American Society: A Record of Social Aspiration, 1607–1937*. New York: Charles Scribner's Sons, 1937.

Wilson, Mrs. Henry Lumpkin. *The Atlanta Exposition Cookbook* 1895. Reprint, Athens: The University of Georgia Press, 1984.

I N D E X